This book belongs to.......

....

....

Small preview of what's inside

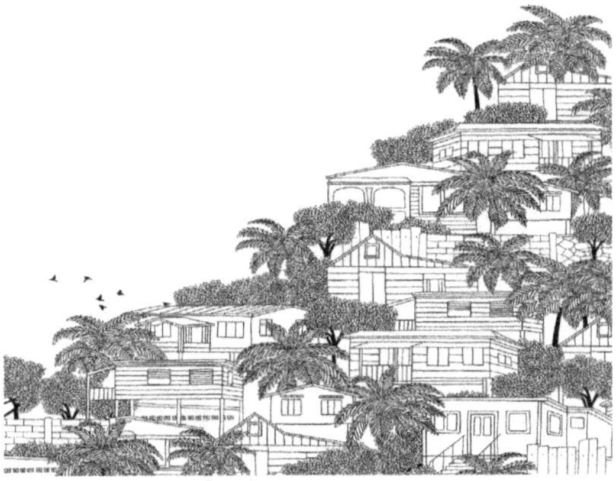

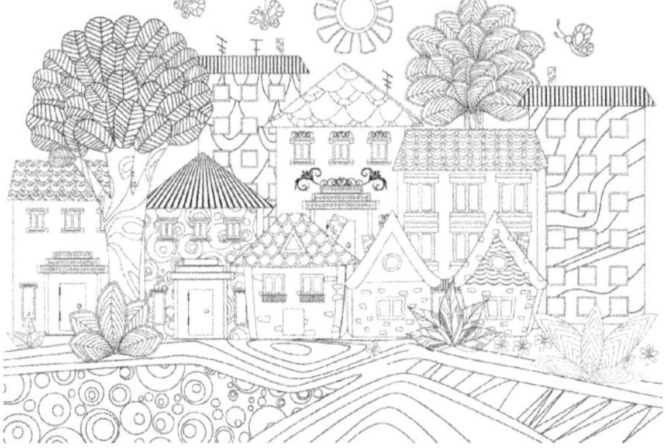

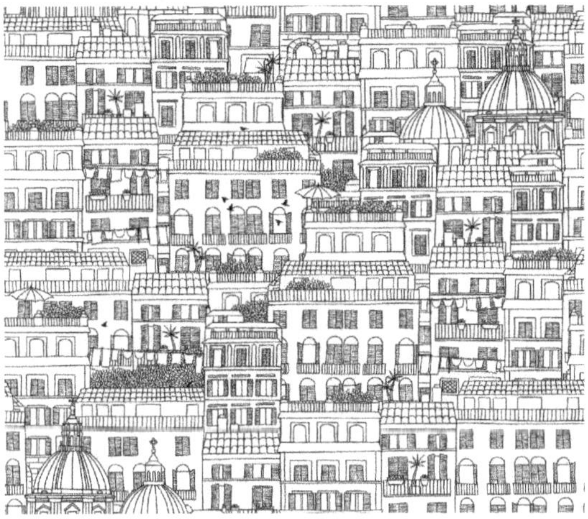

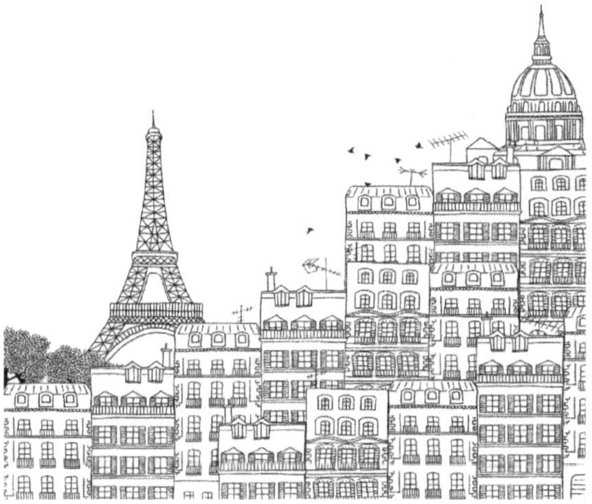

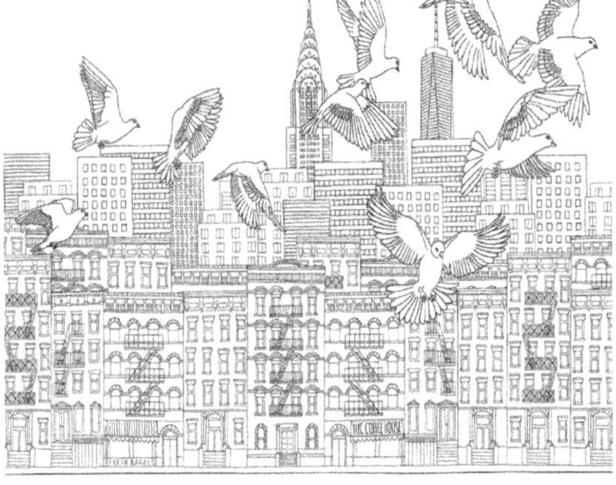

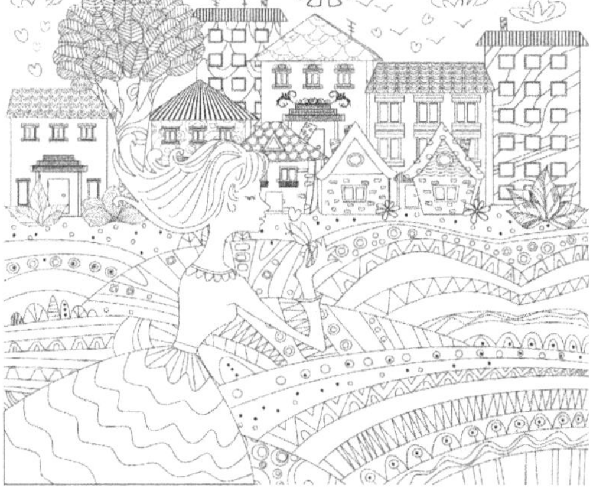

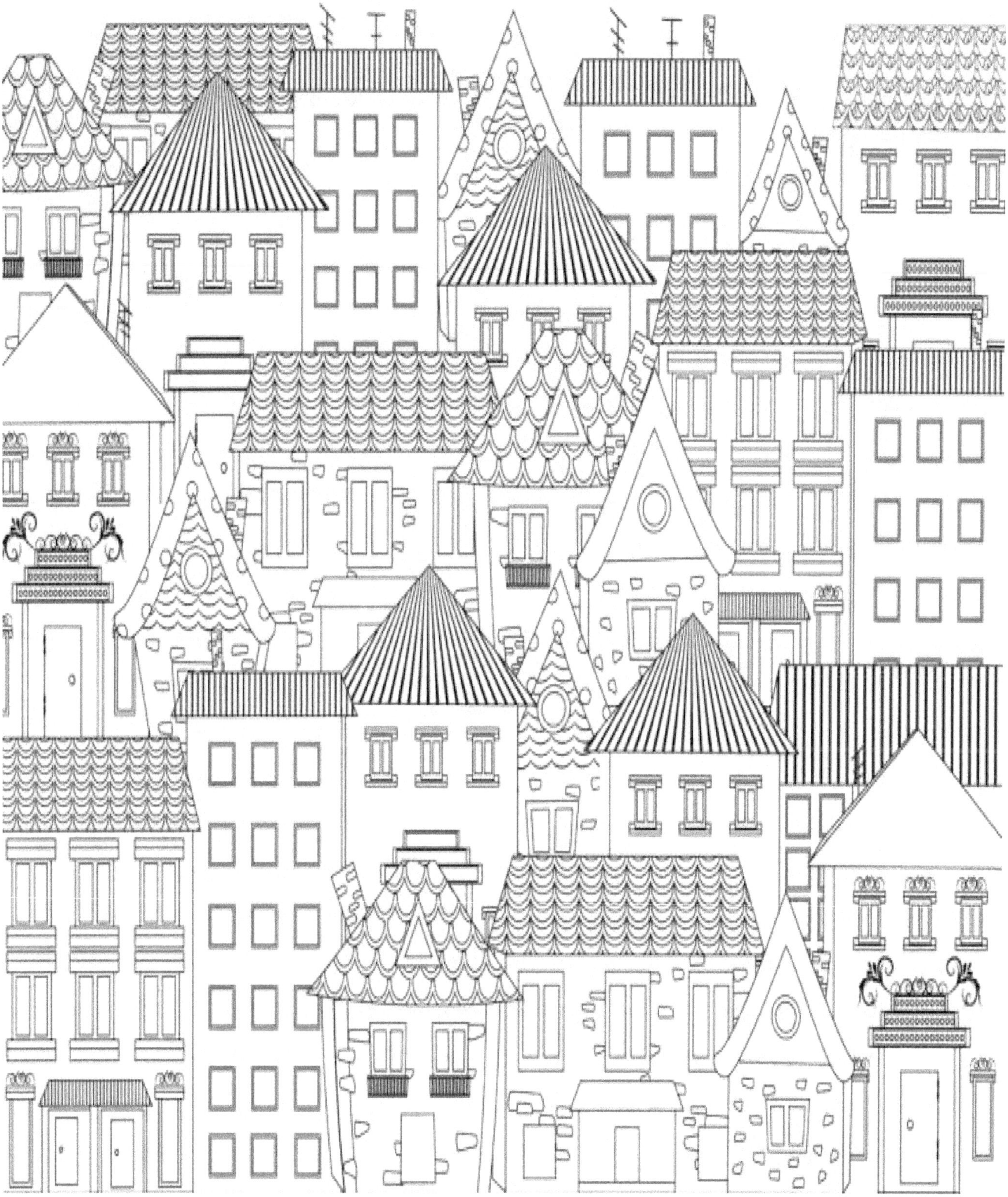

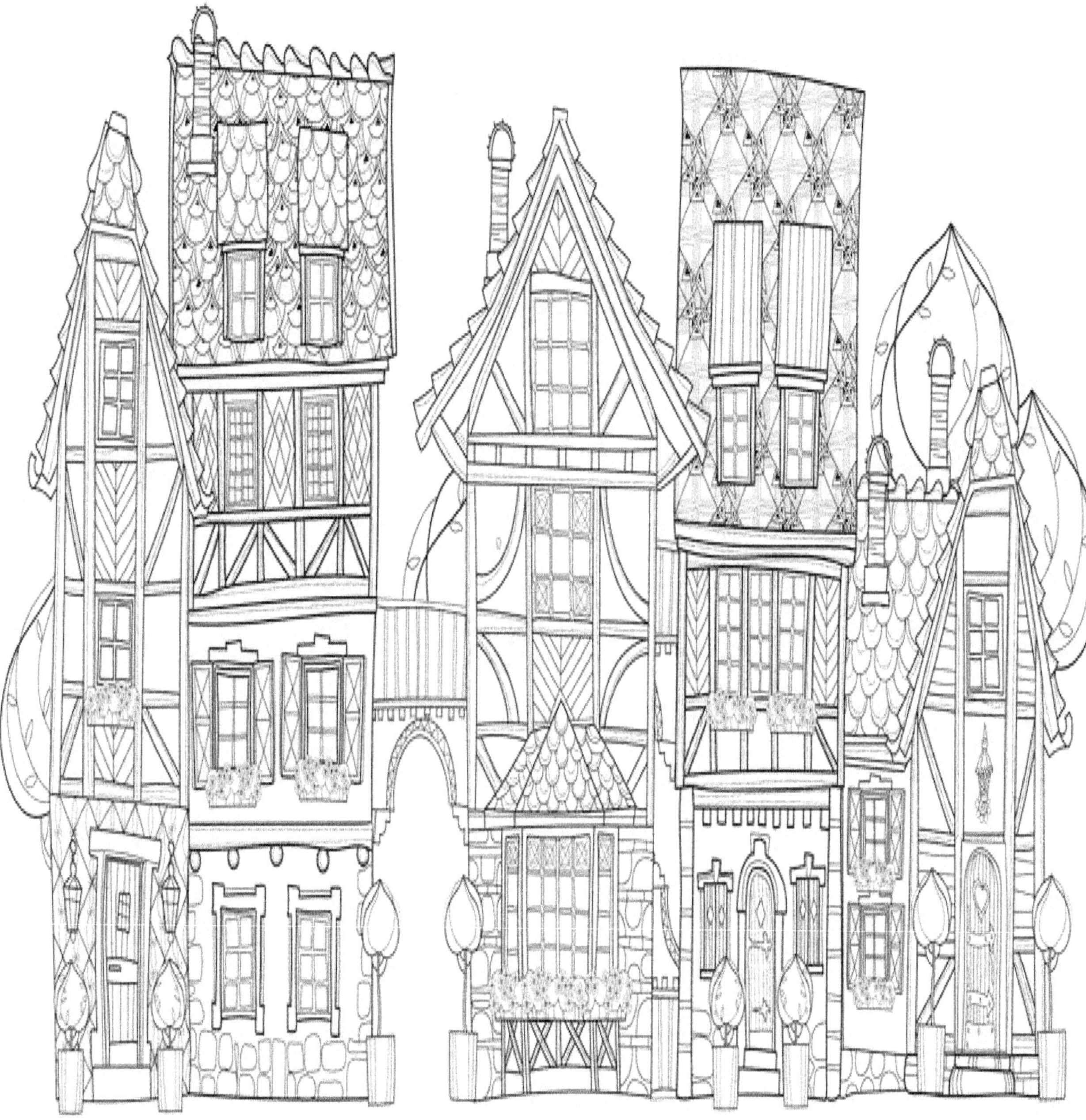

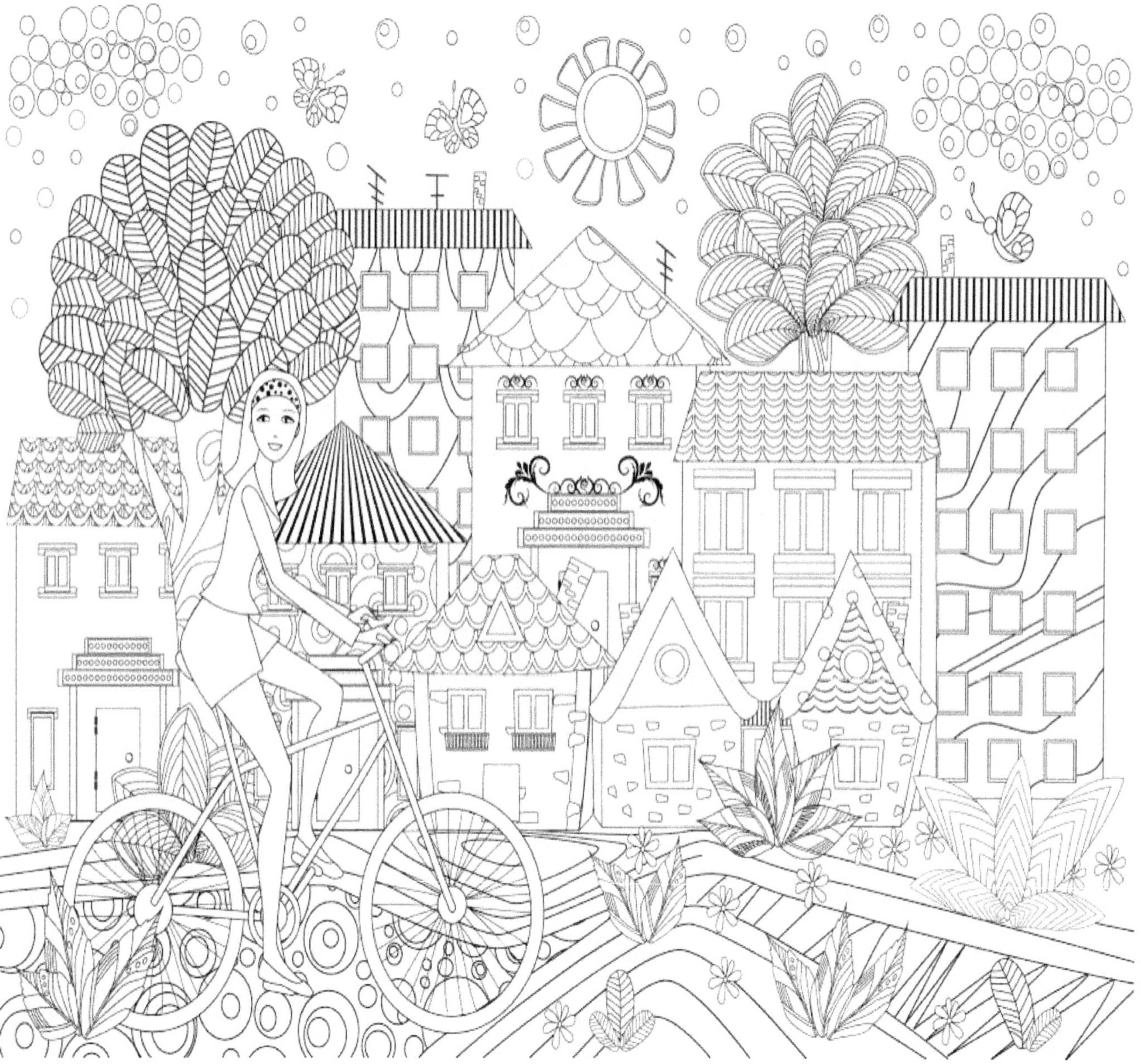

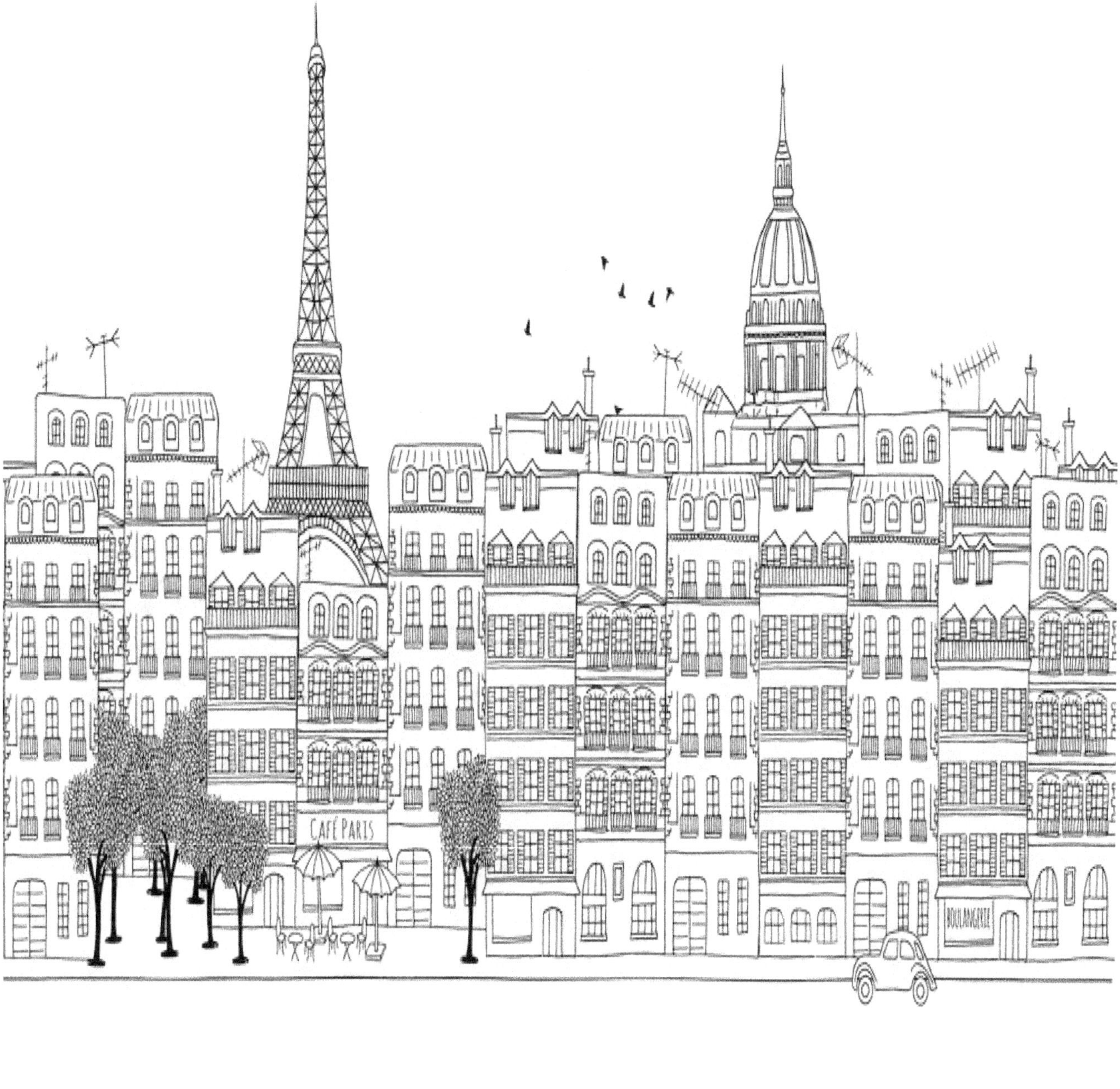
CAFÉ PARIS
BOULANGERIE

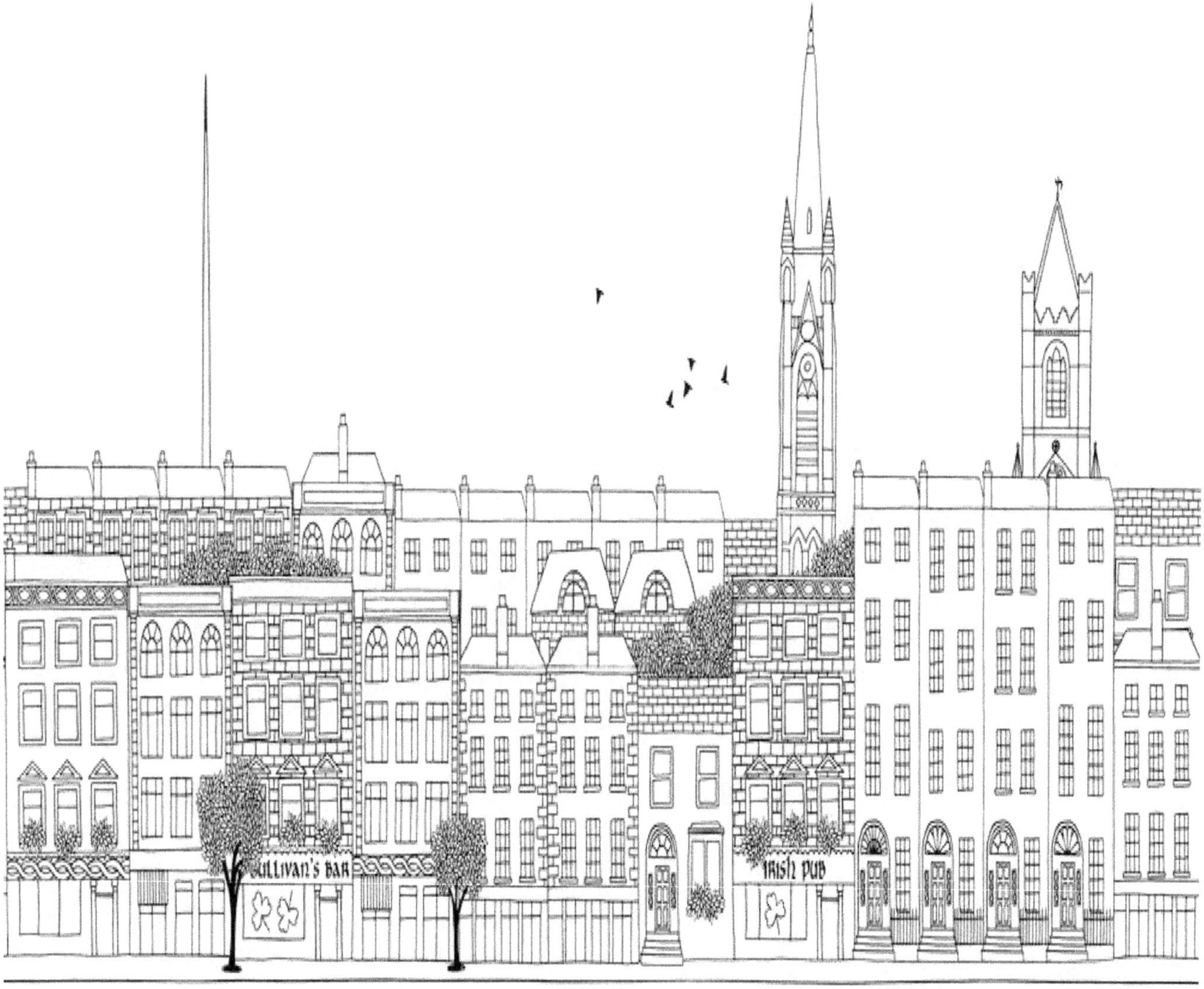
ULLIVAN'S BAR
IRISH PUB

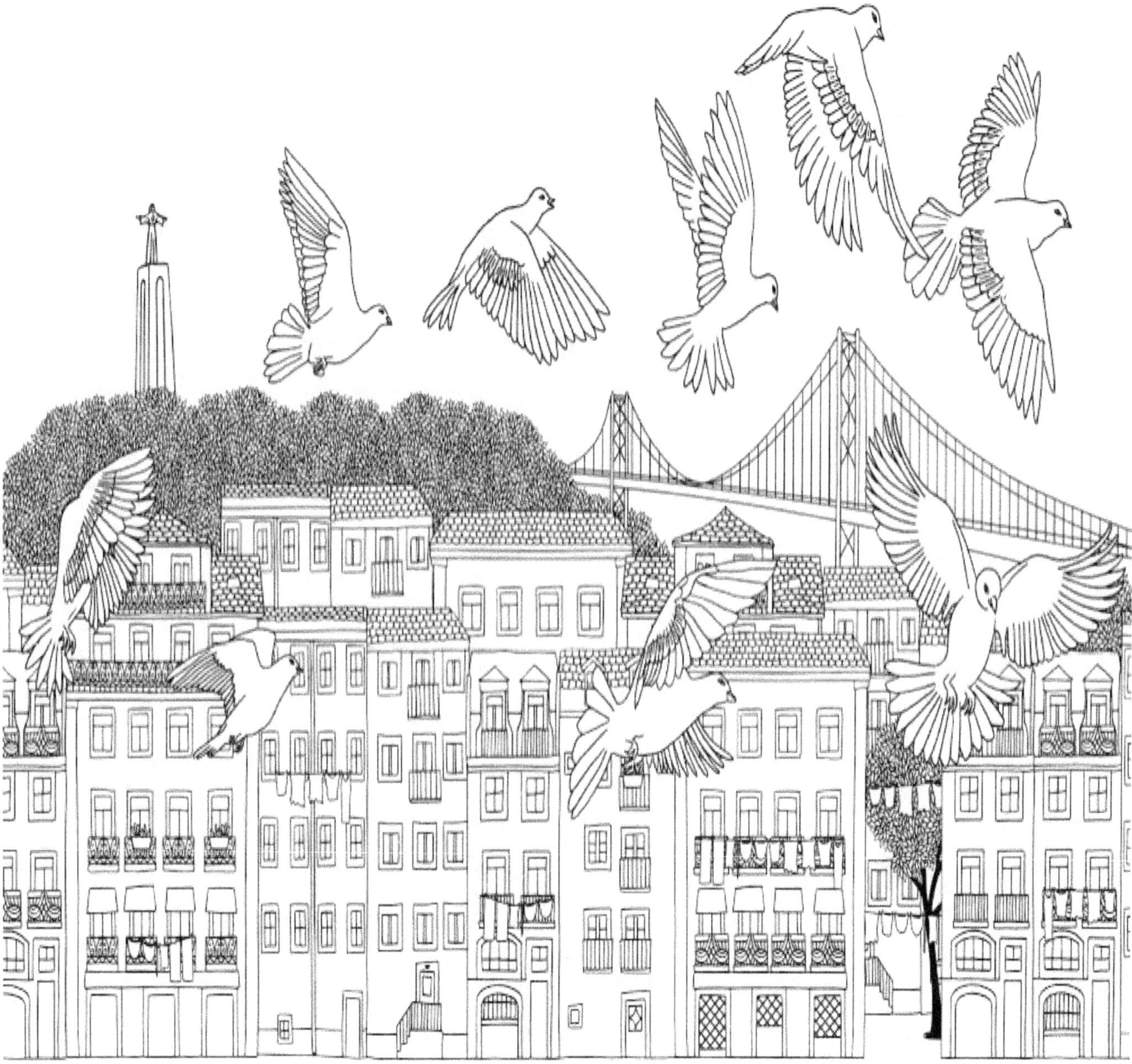

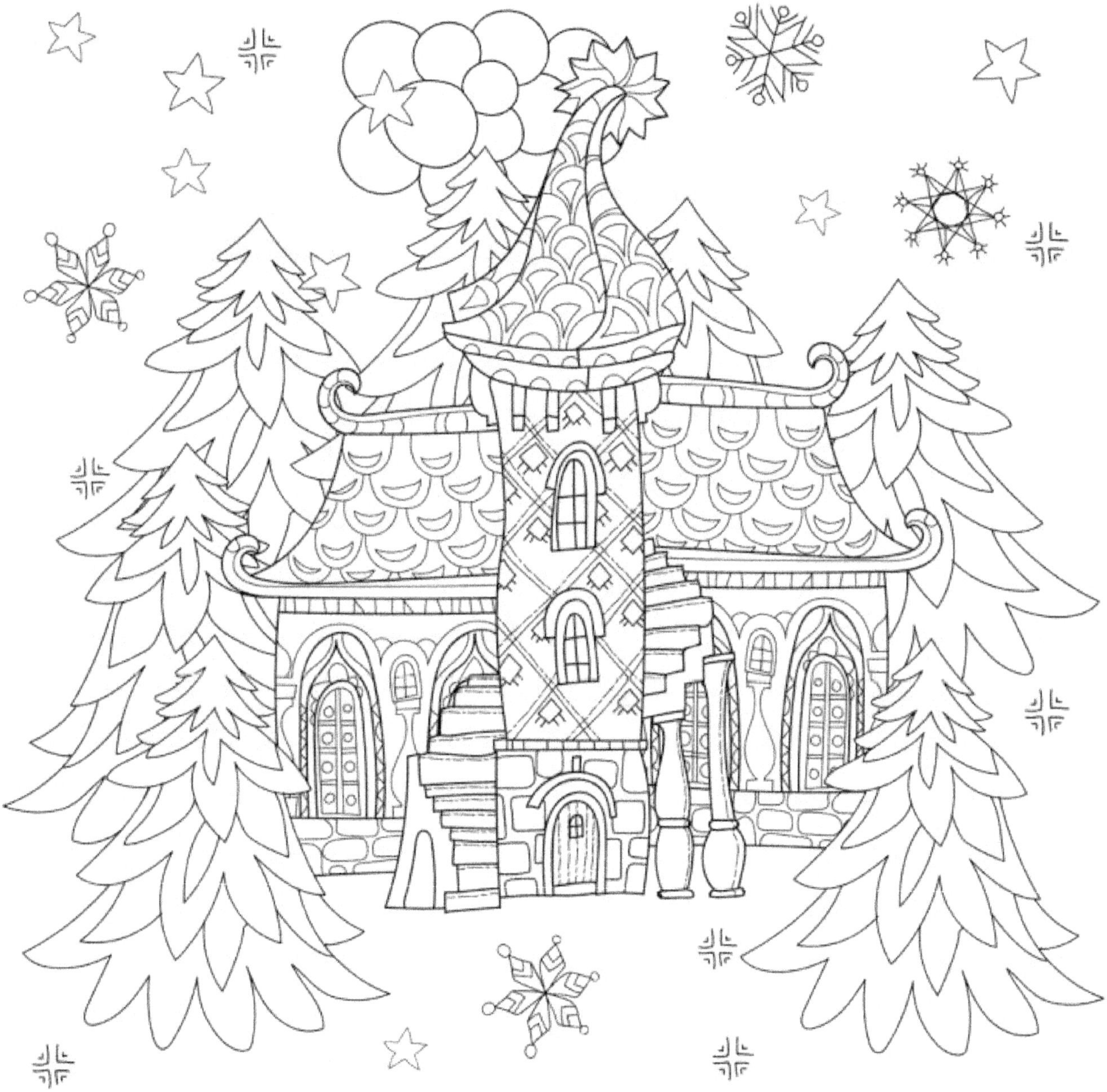

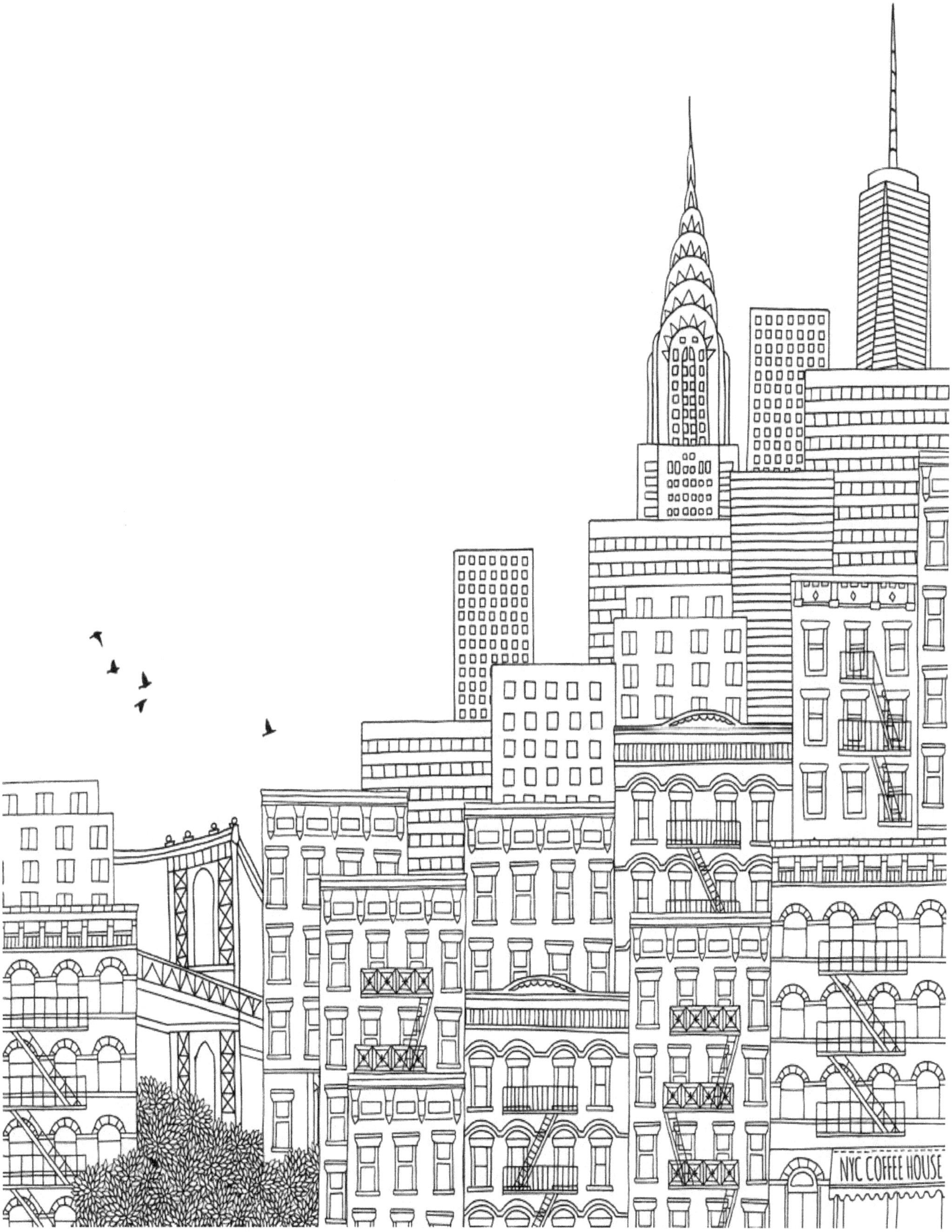
NYC COFFEE HOUSE

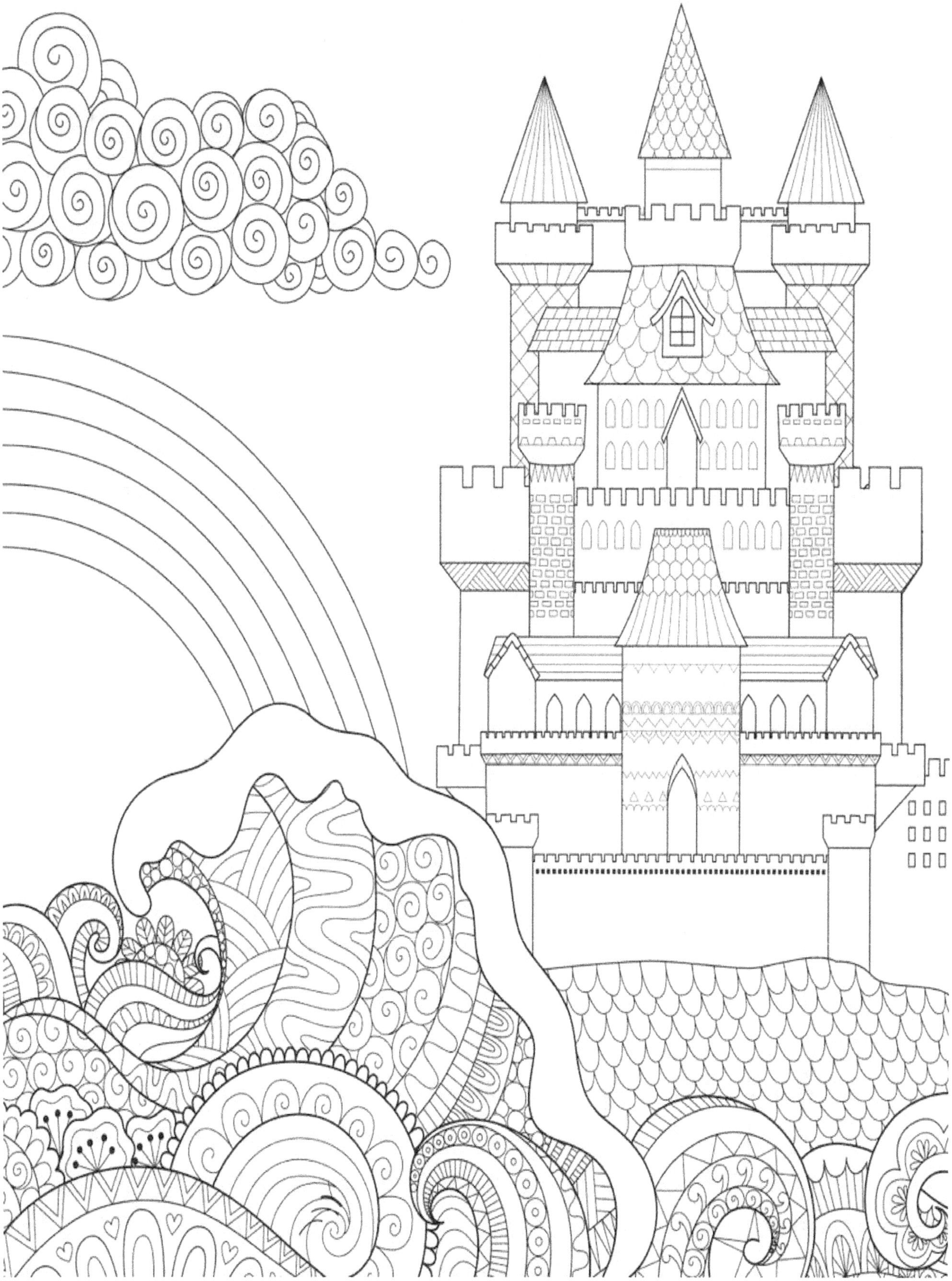

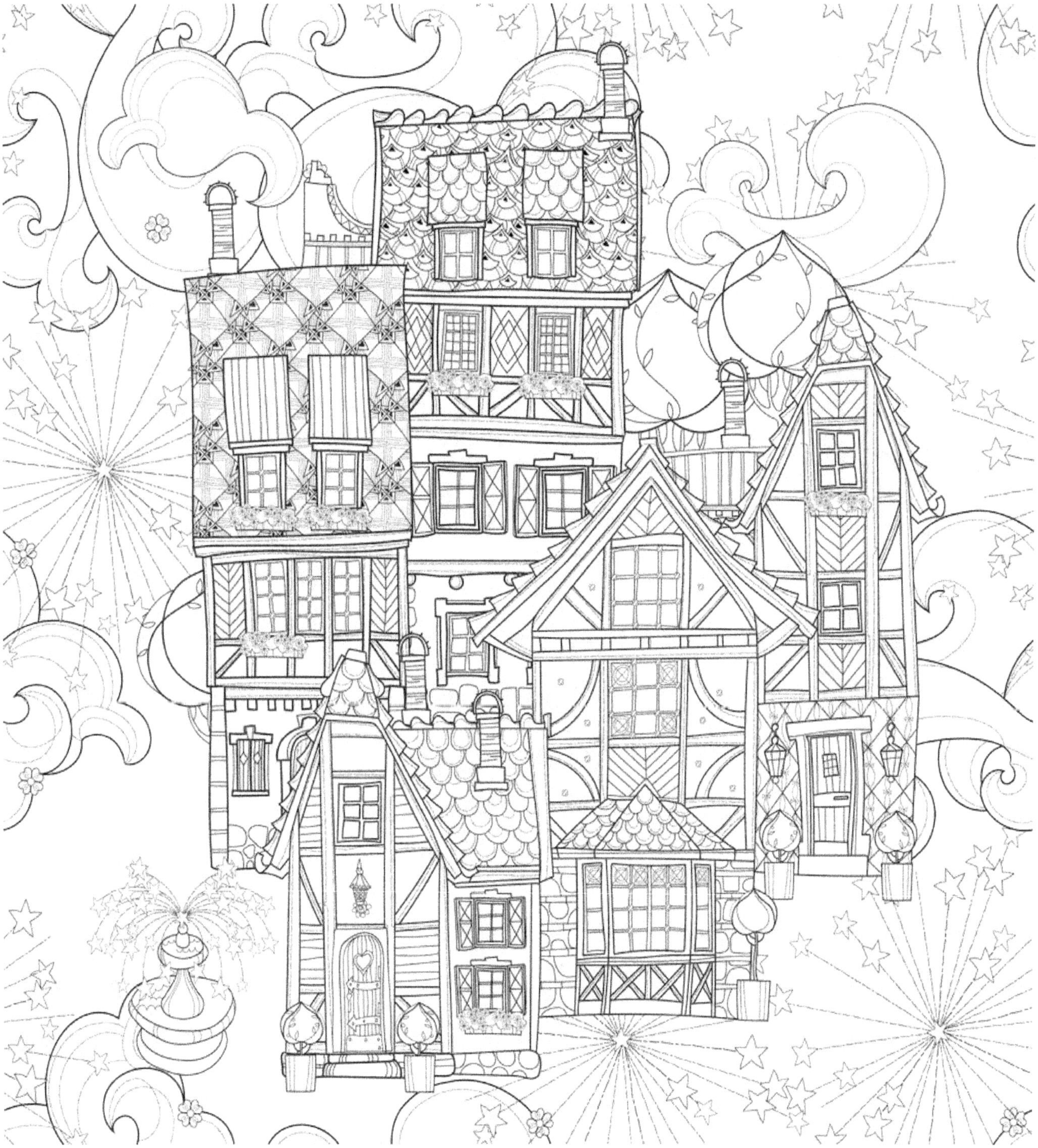

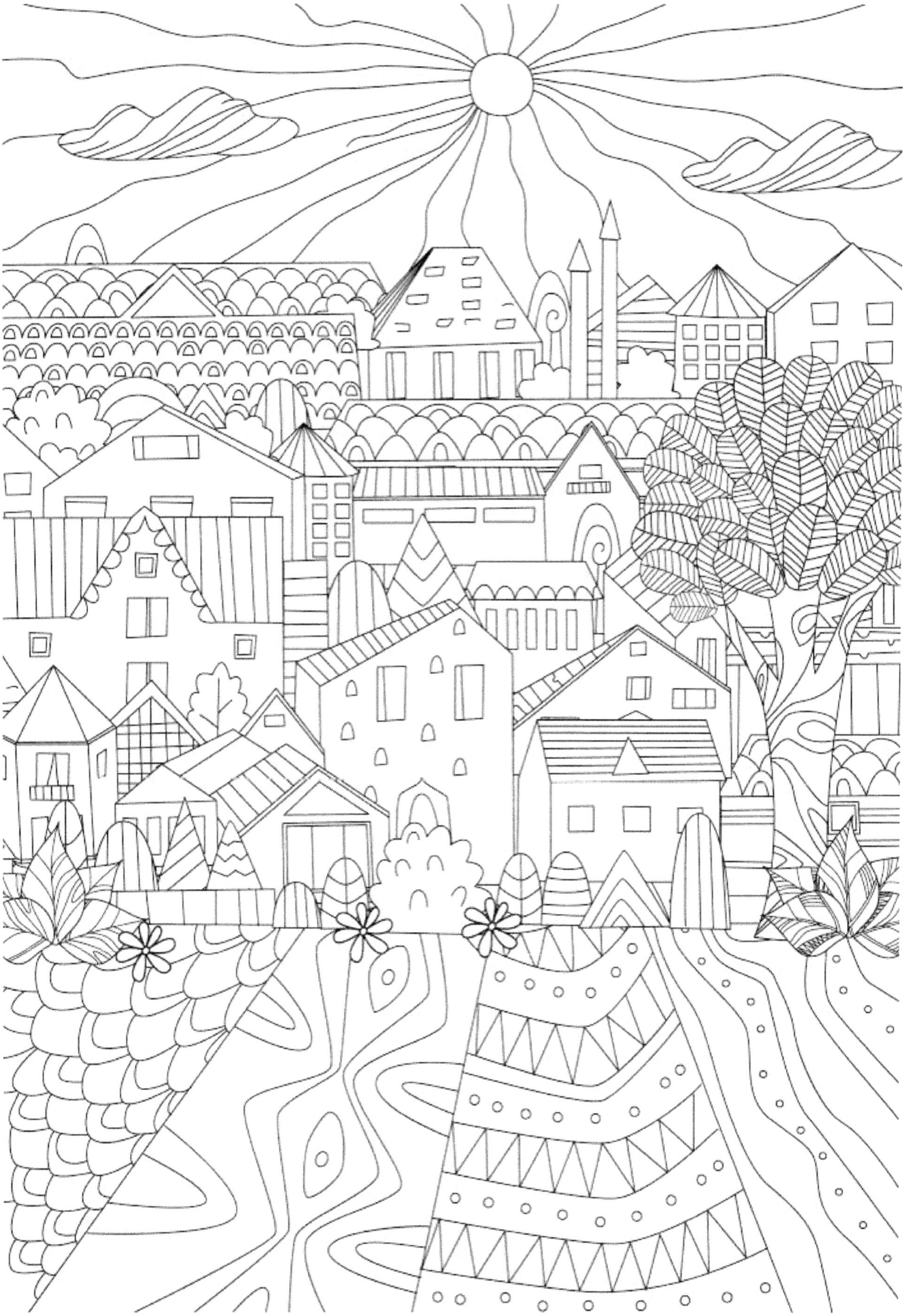

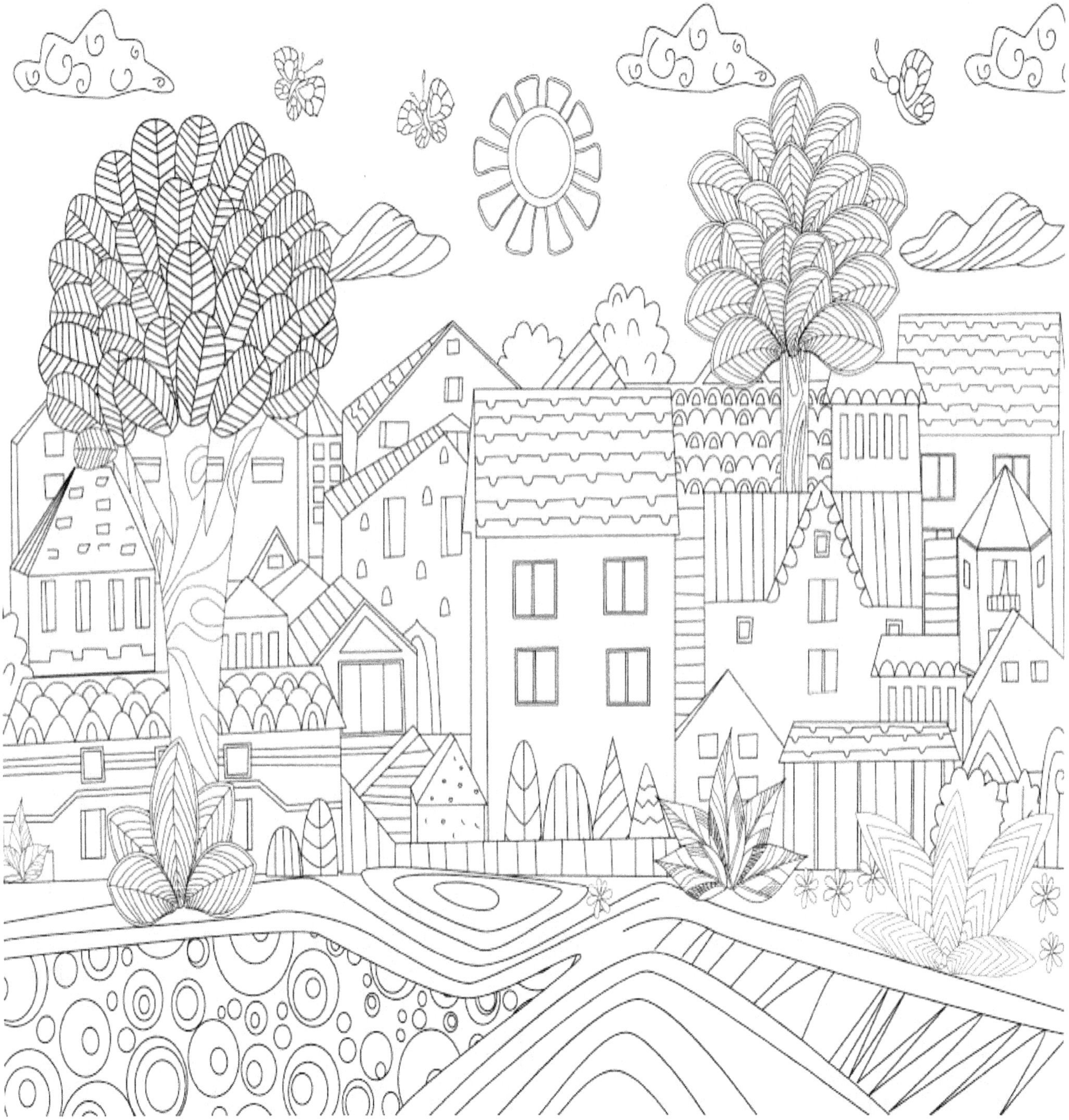

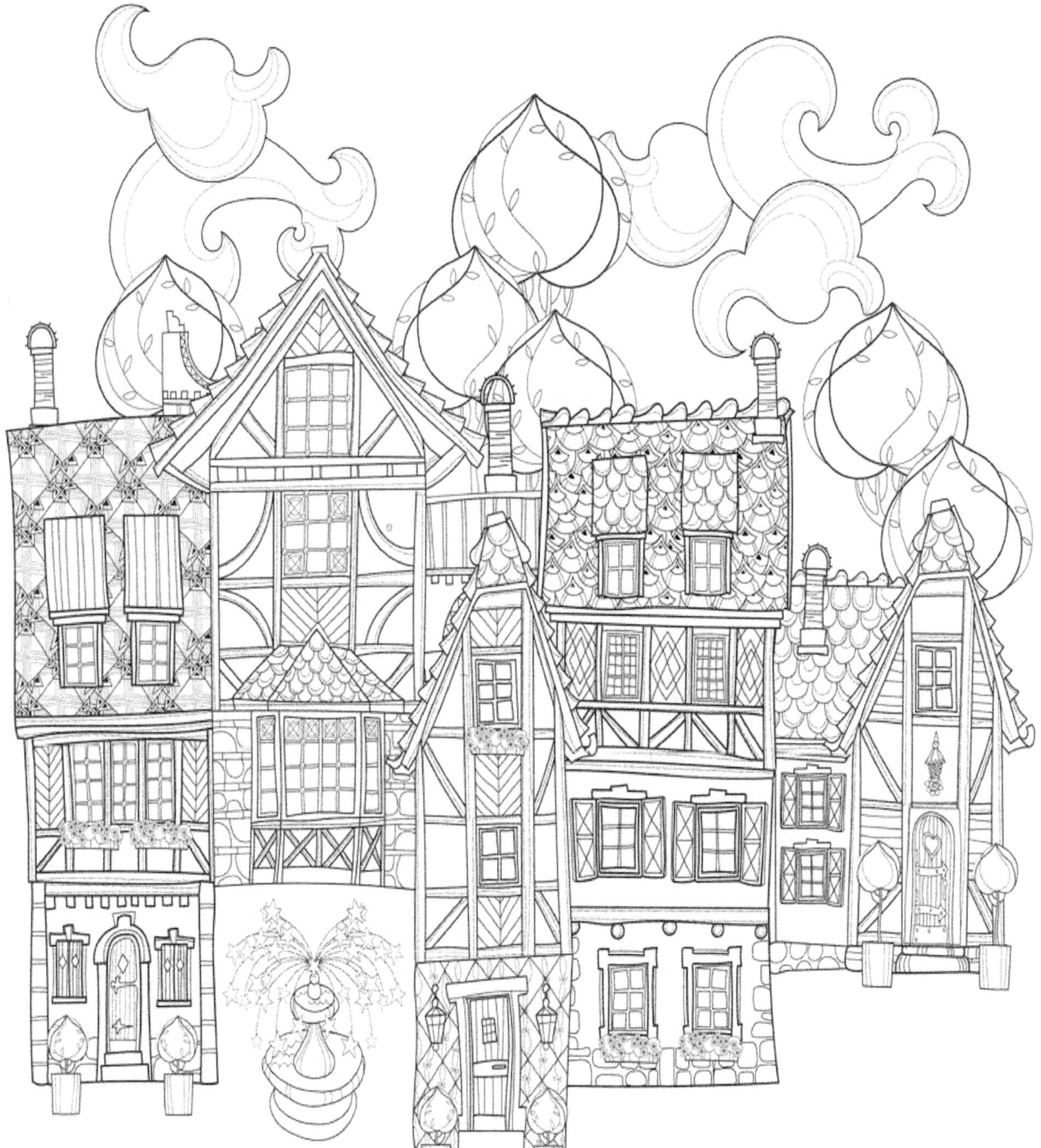

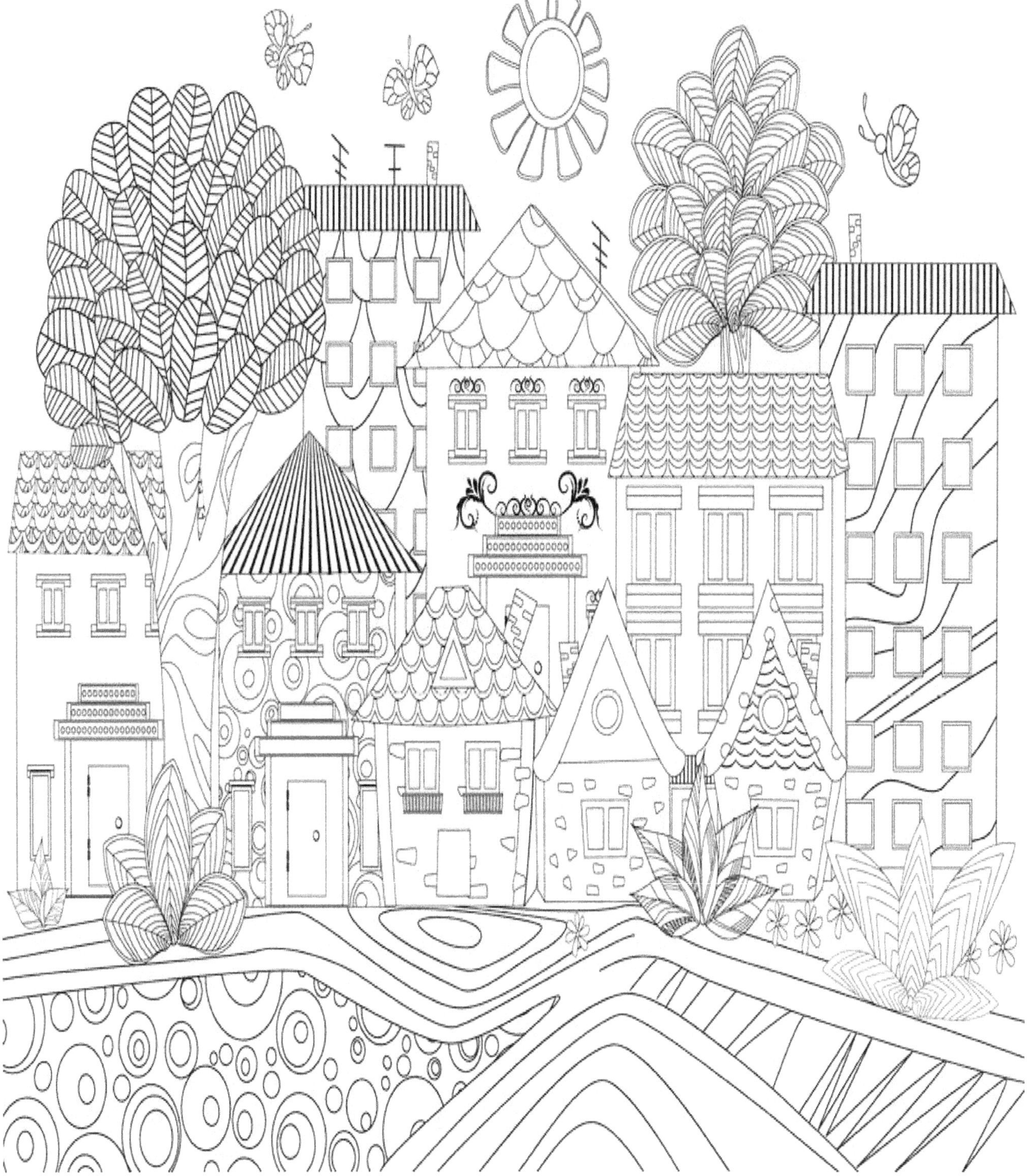

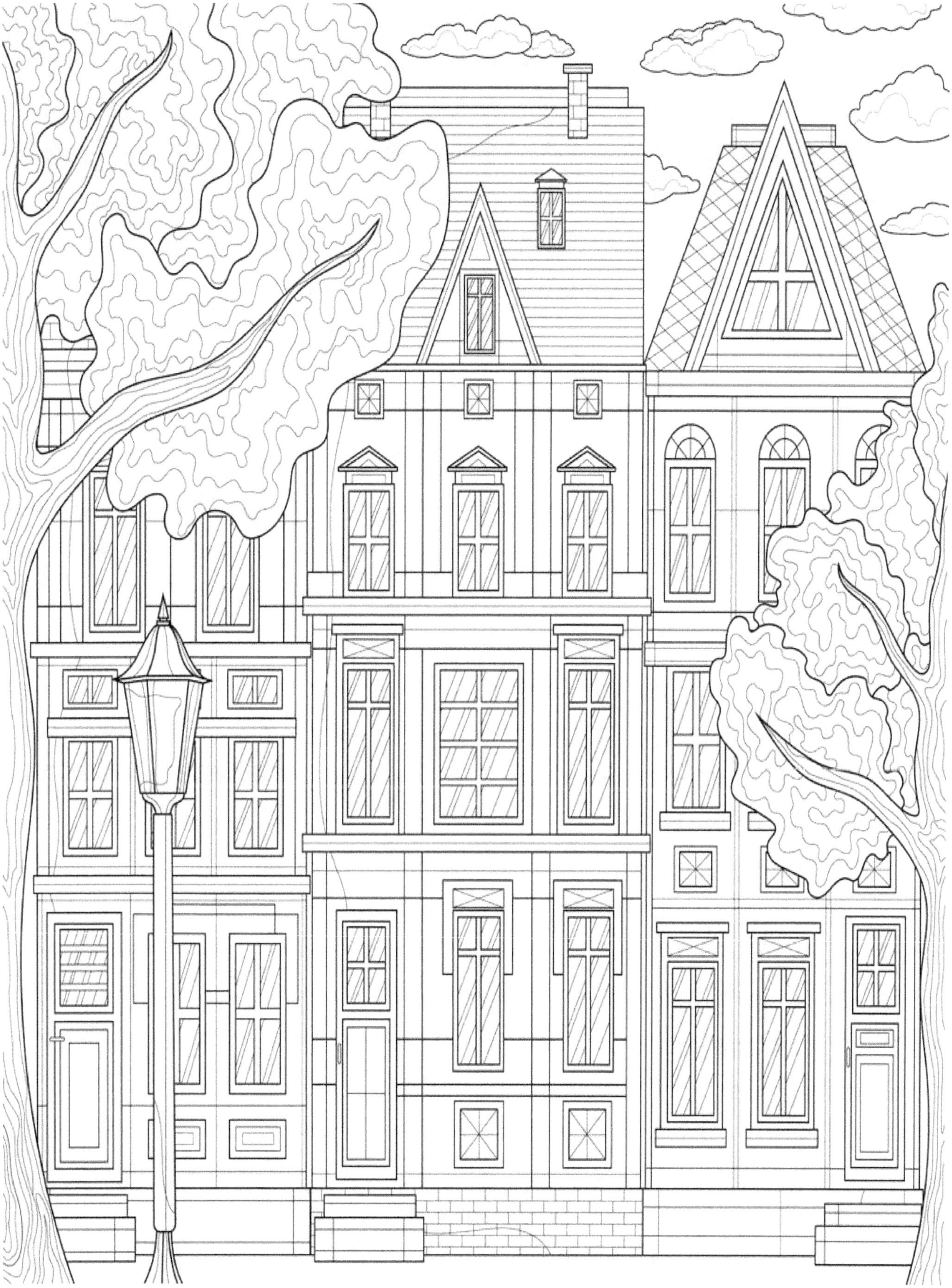

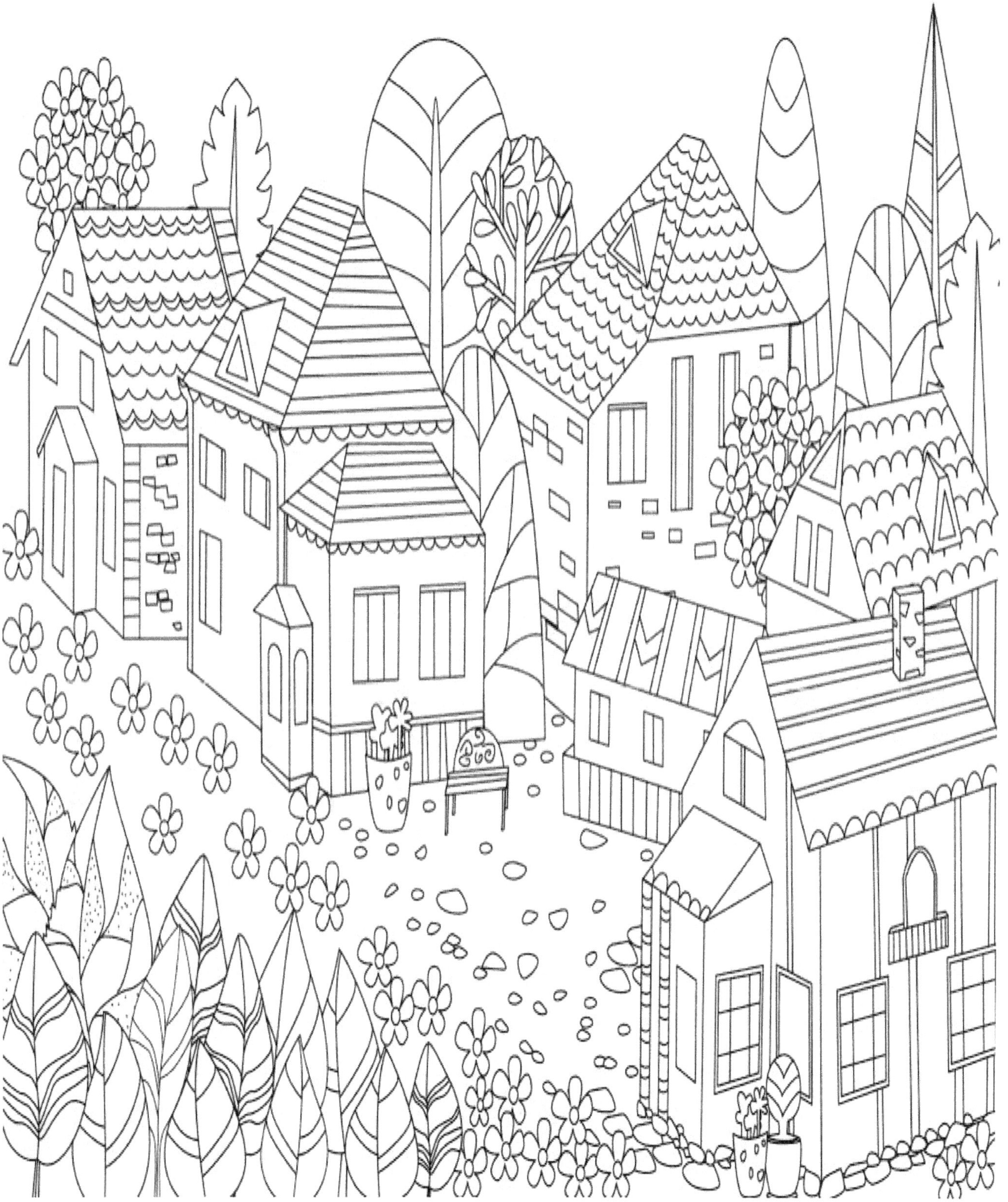

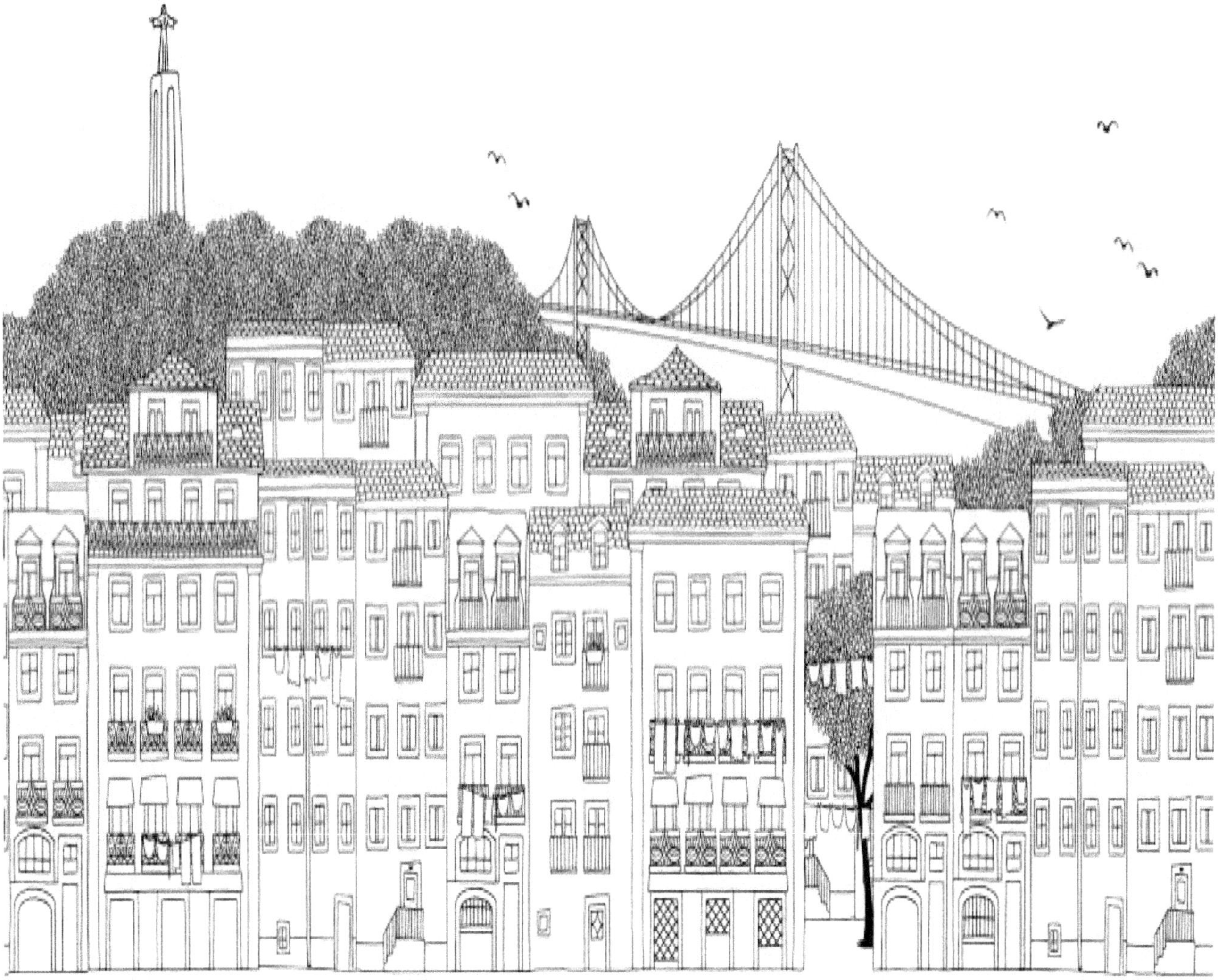

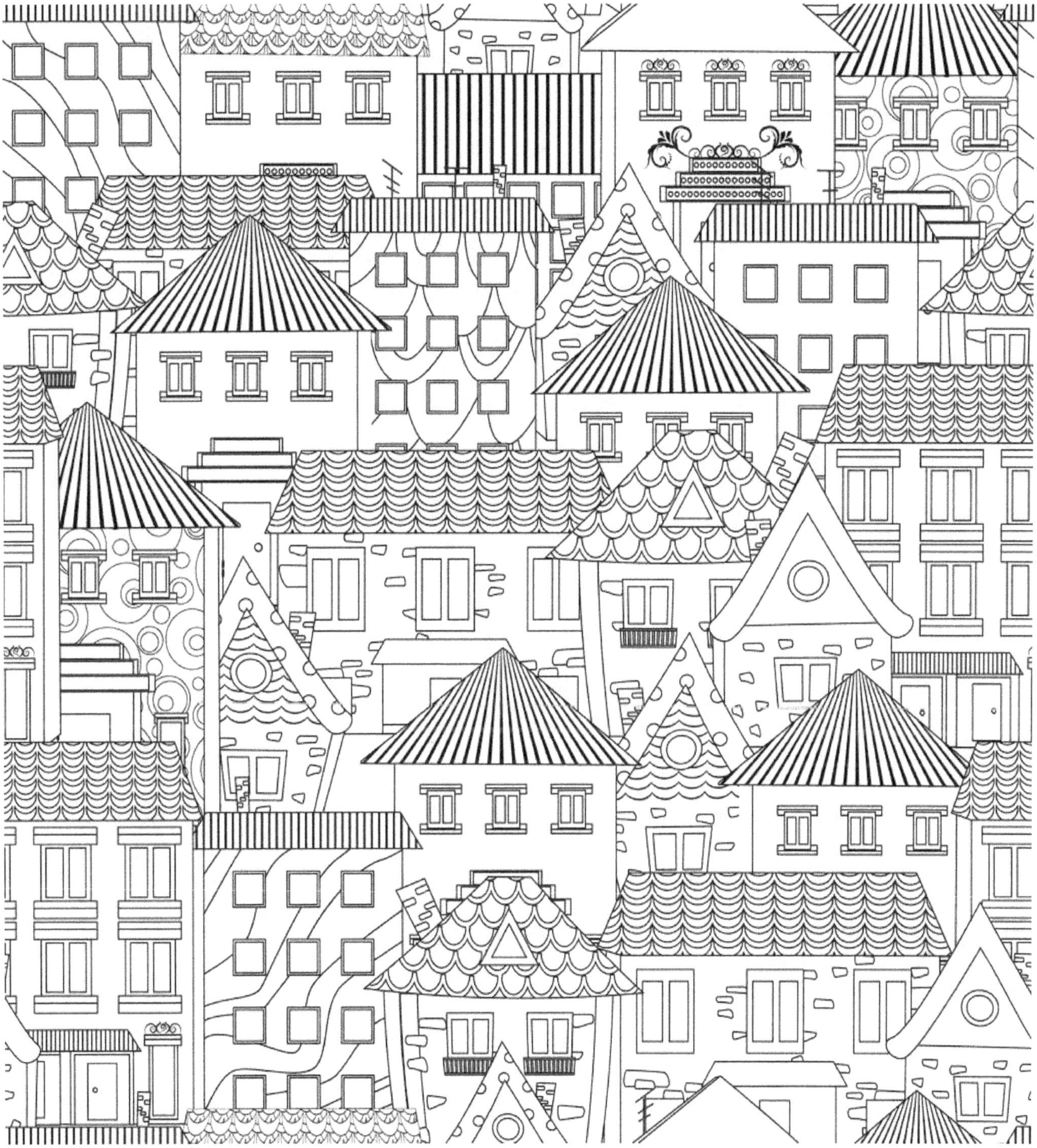

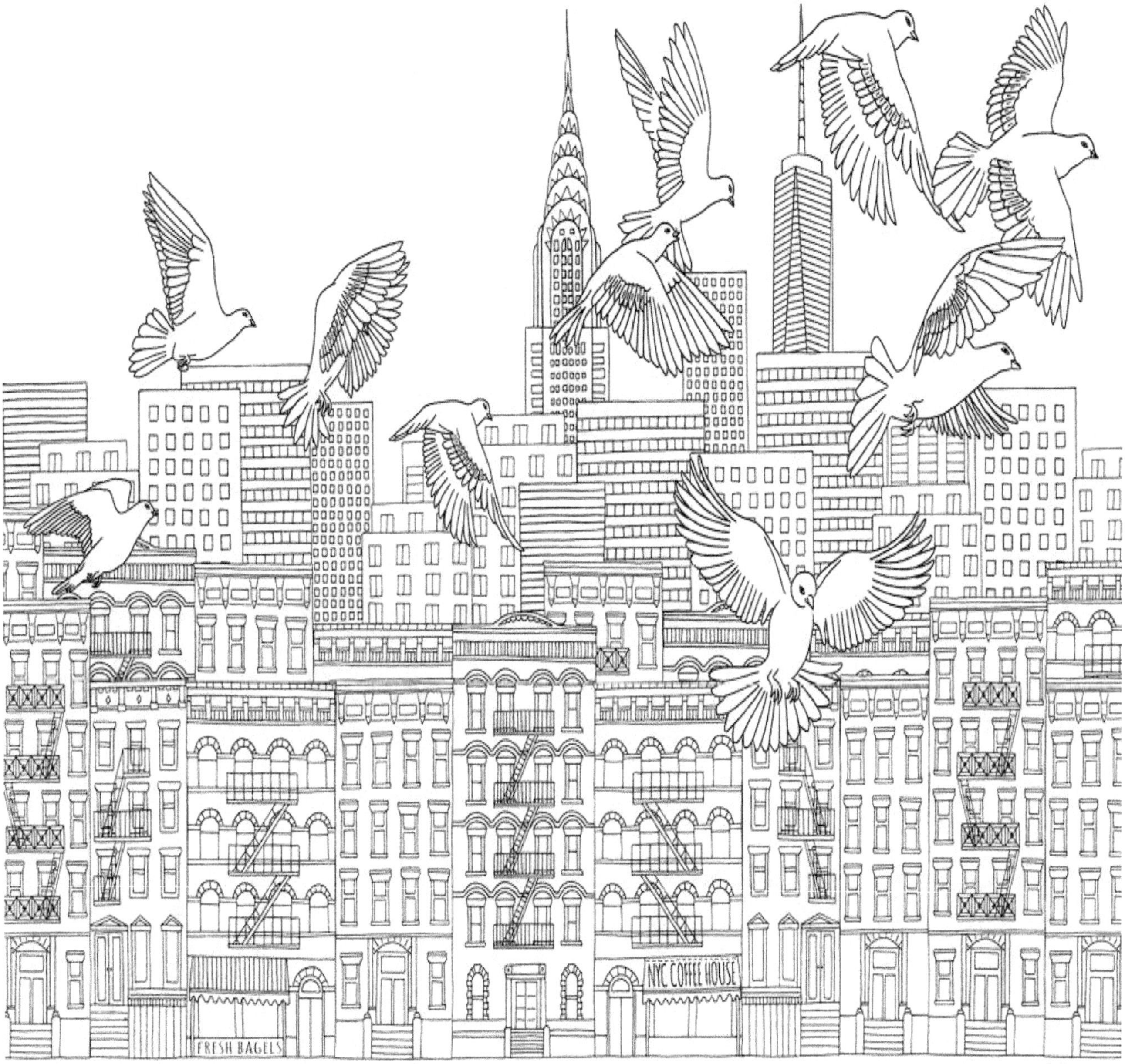
NYC COFFEE HOUSE
FRESH BAGELS

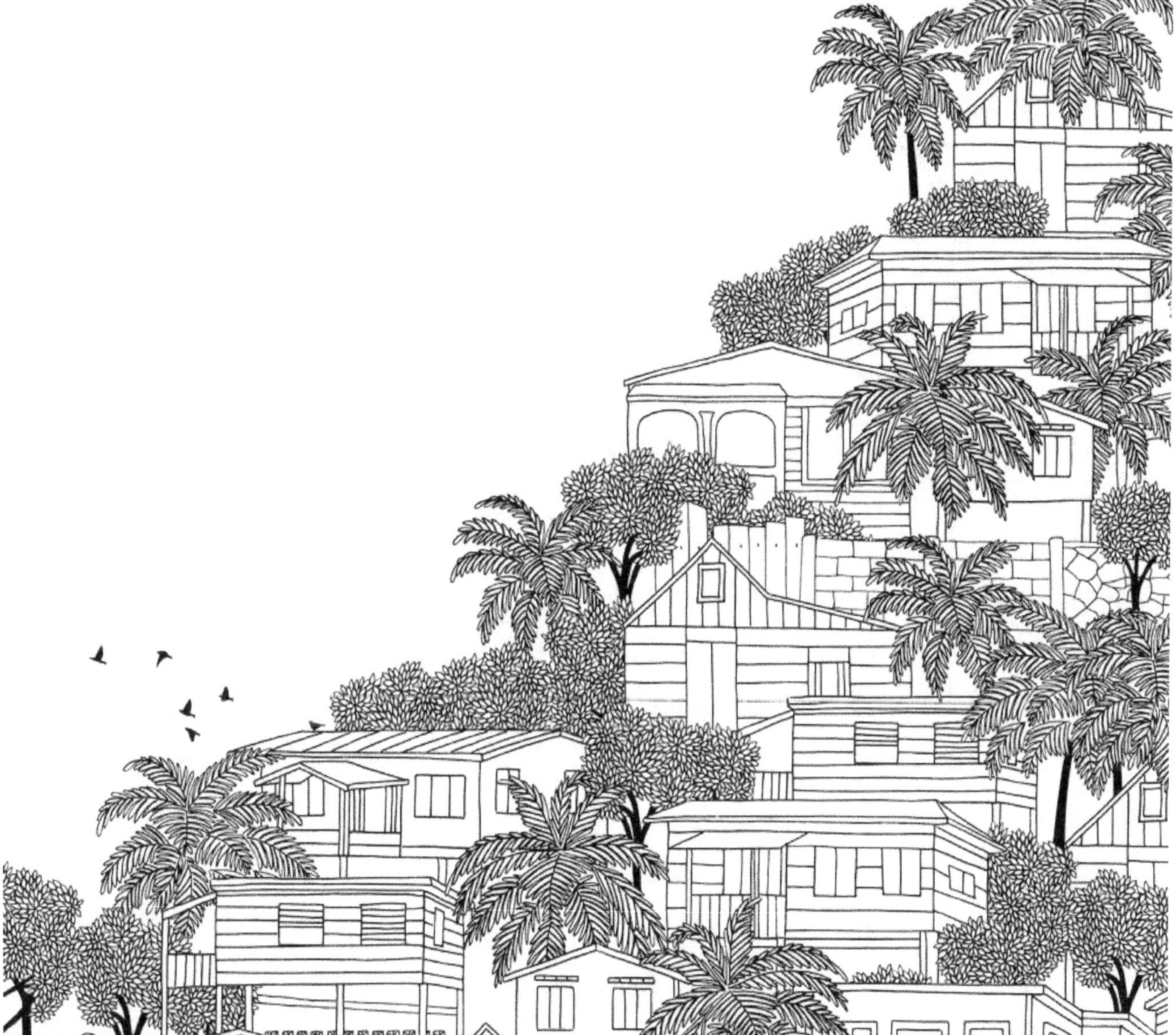

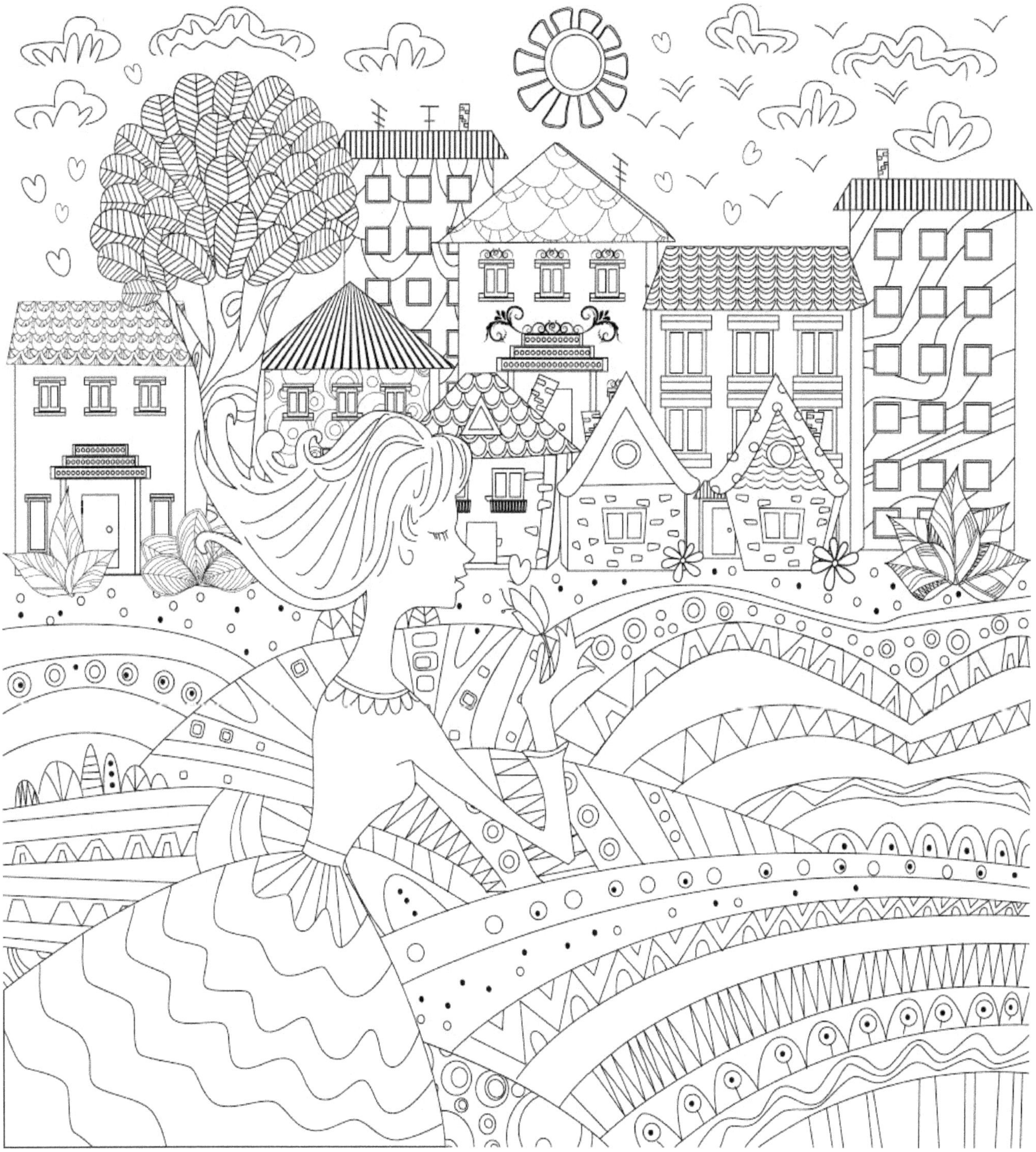

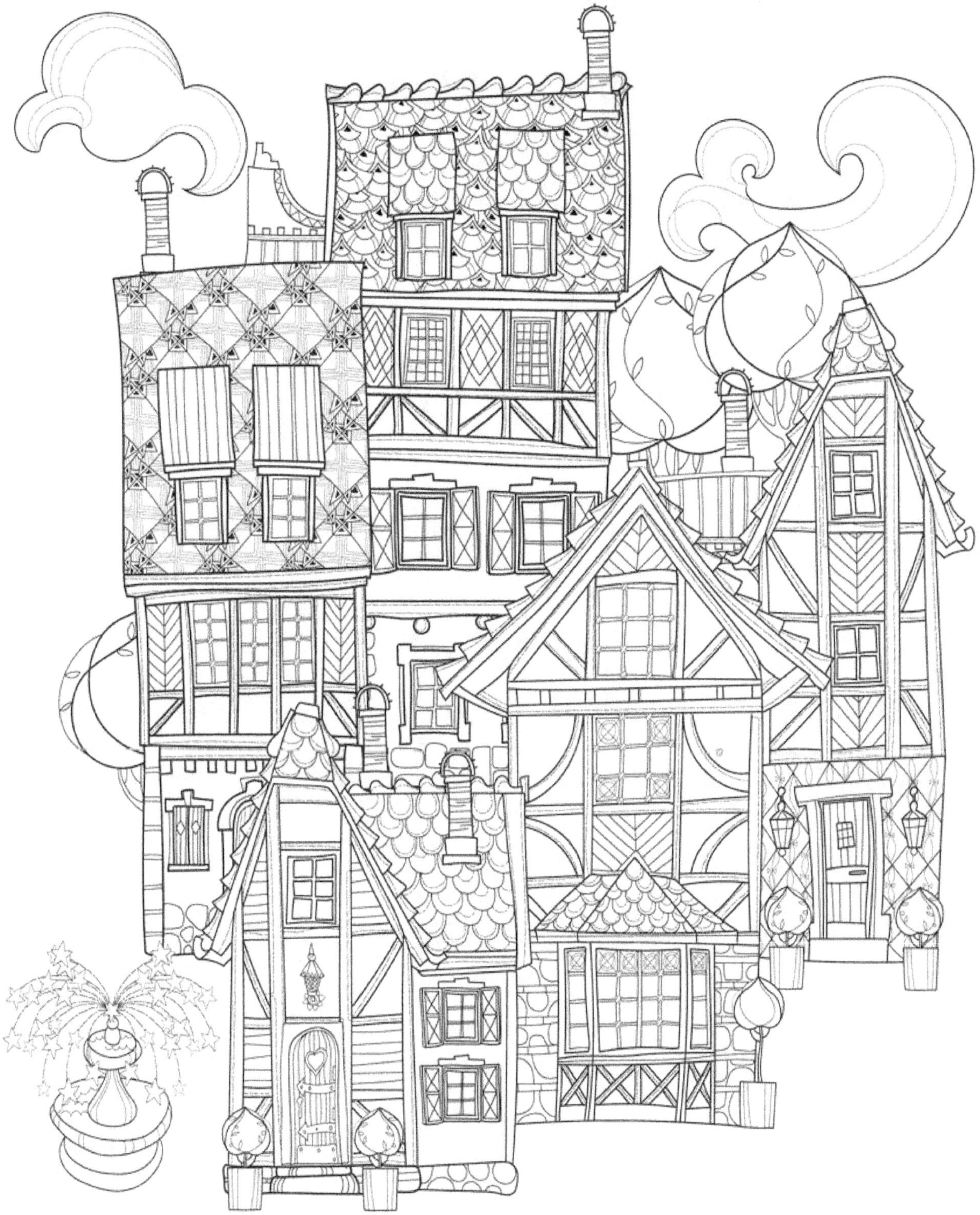

NYC COFFEE HOUSE

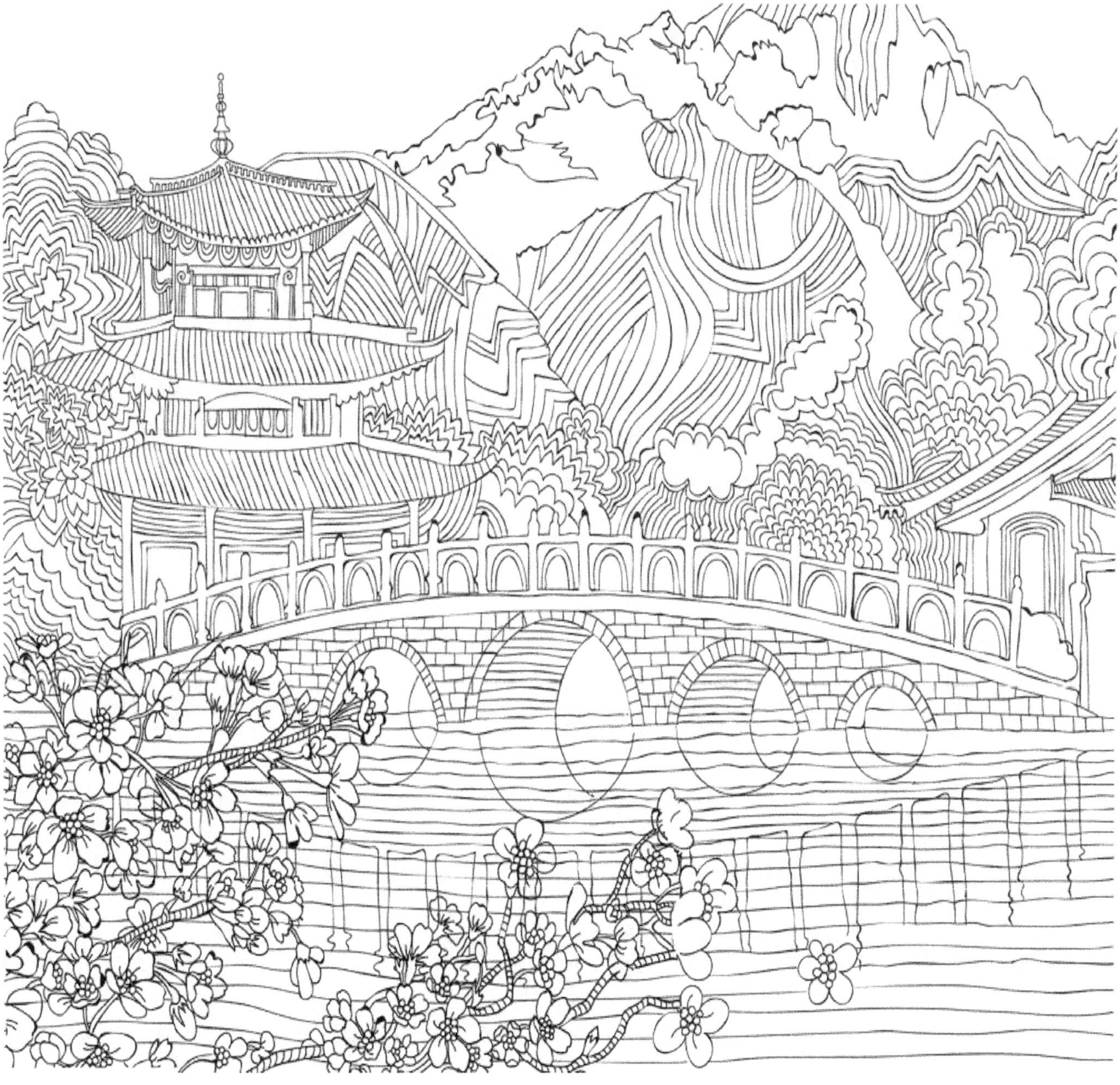

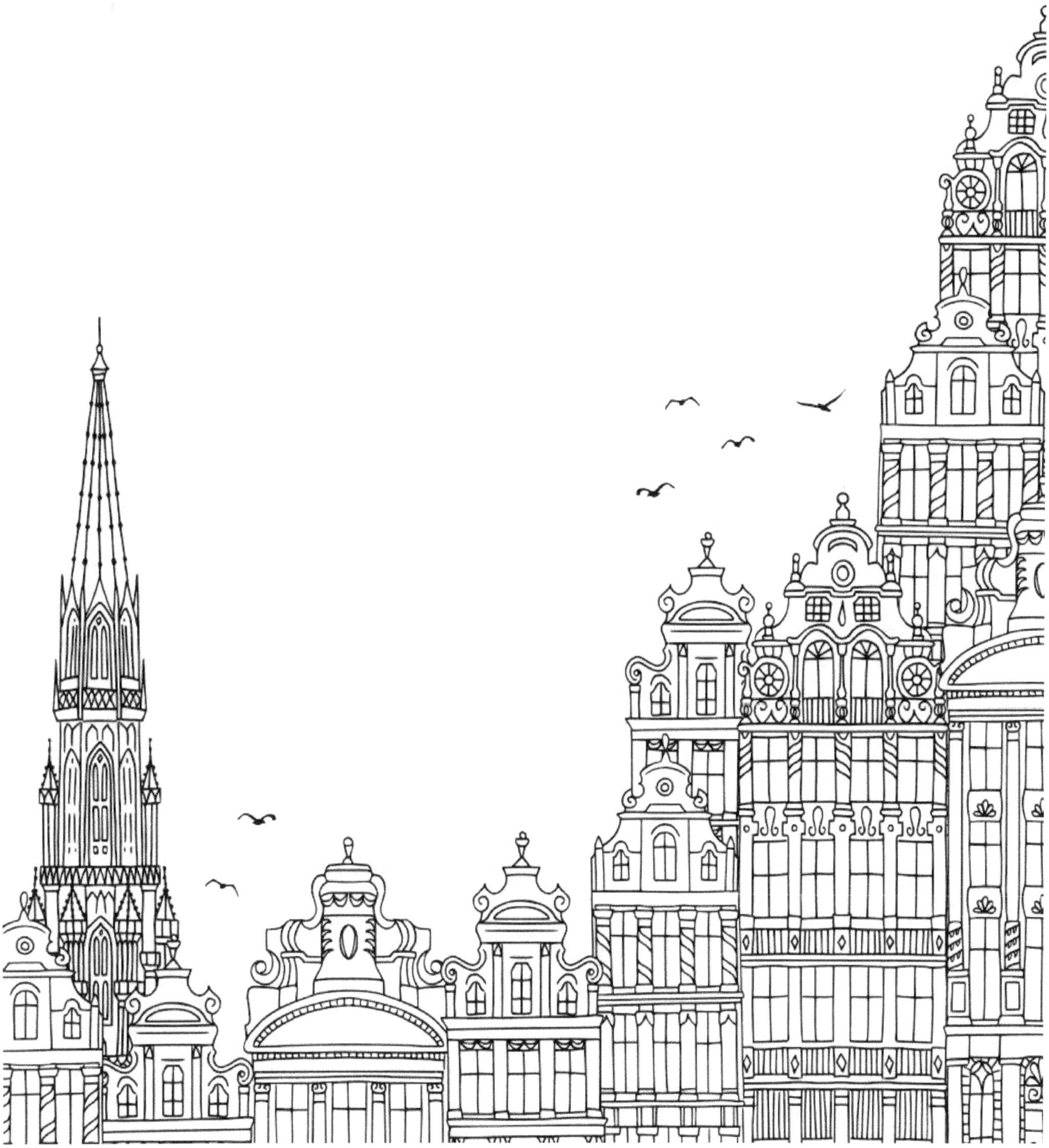

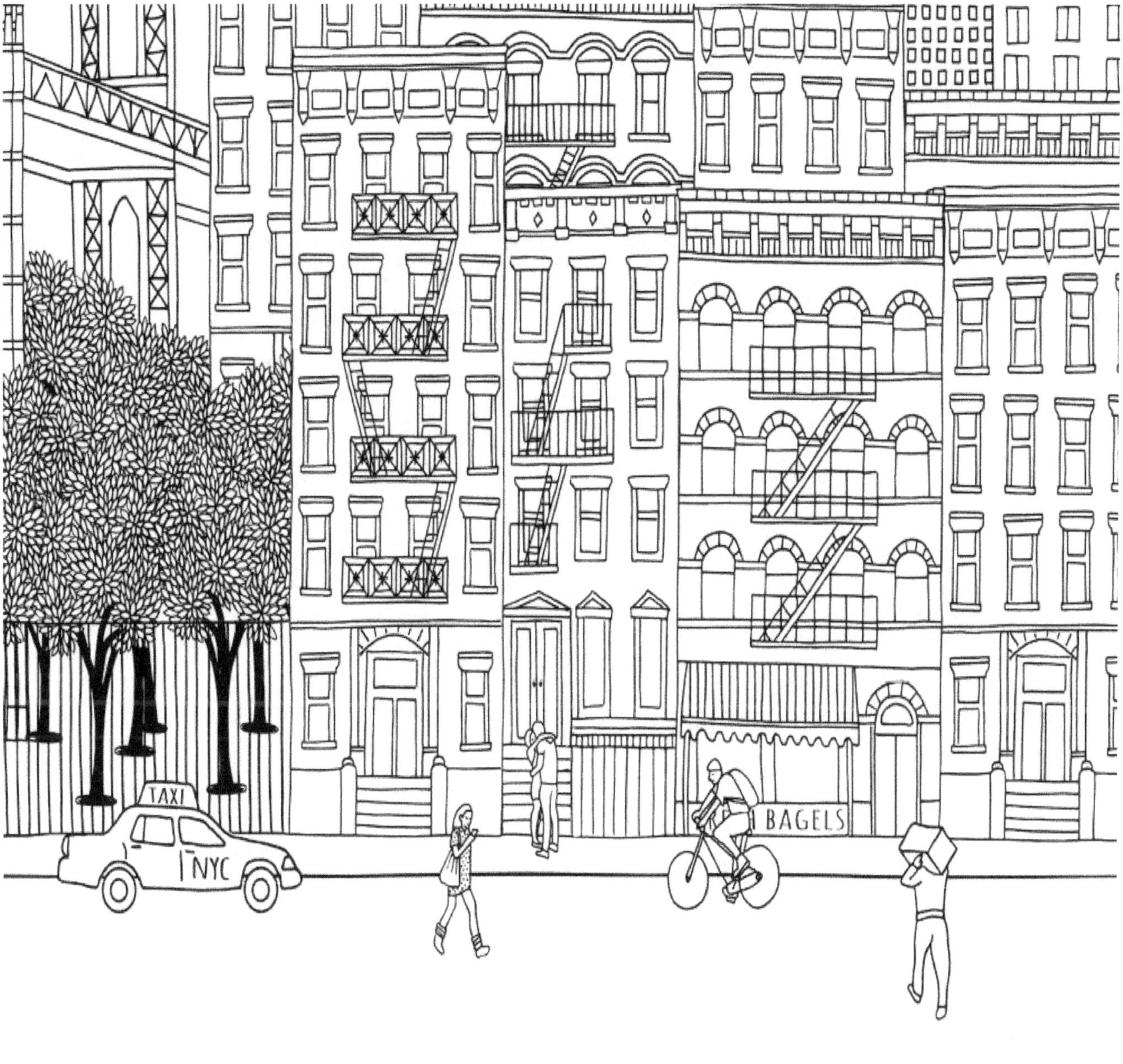
TAXI
NYC
BAGELS

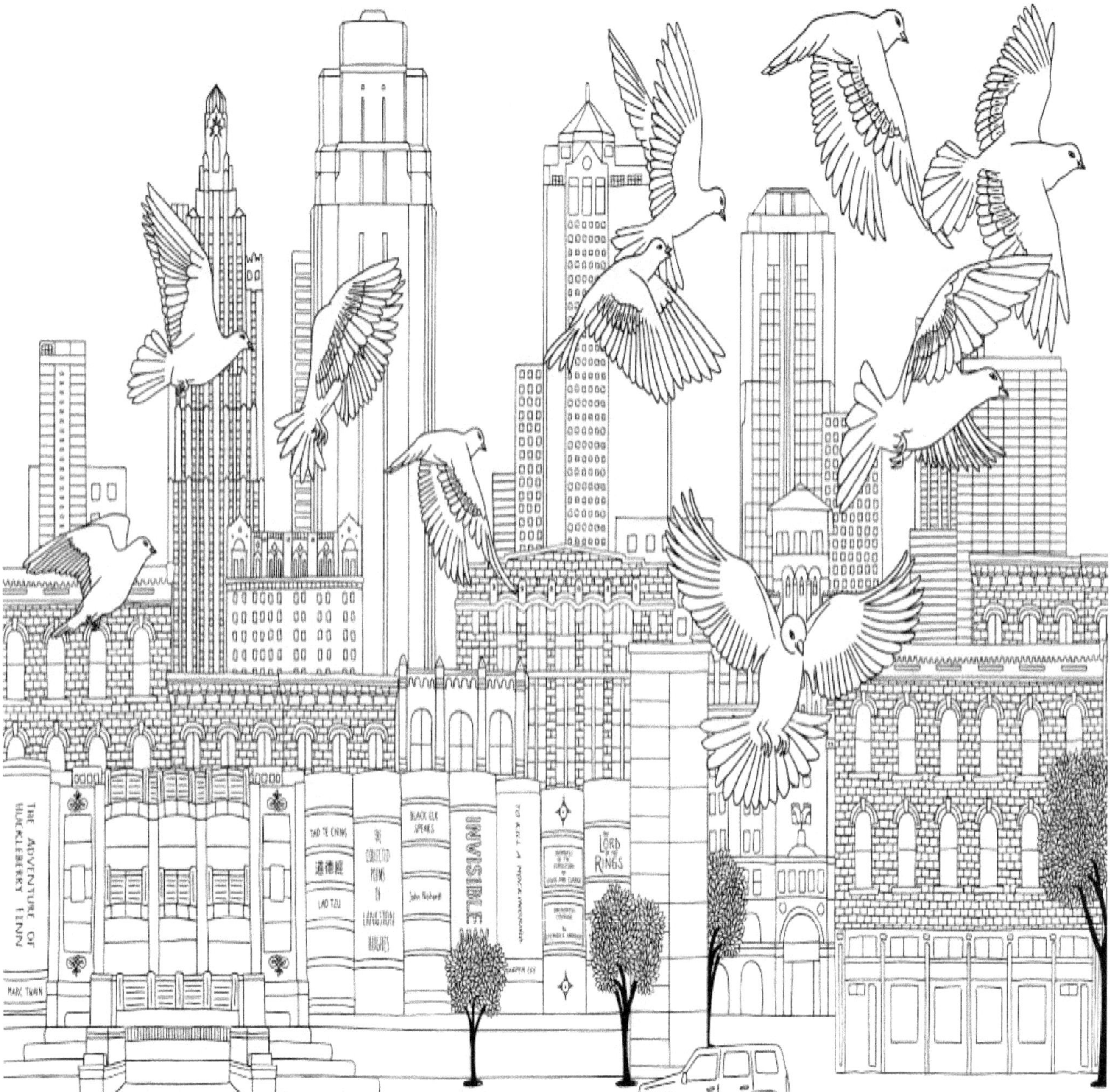
THE ADVENTURE OF HUCKLEBERRY FINN
MARC TWAIN
TAO TE CHING
道德經
LAO TZU
BLACK ELK SPEAKS
INVISIBLE
LORD RINGS

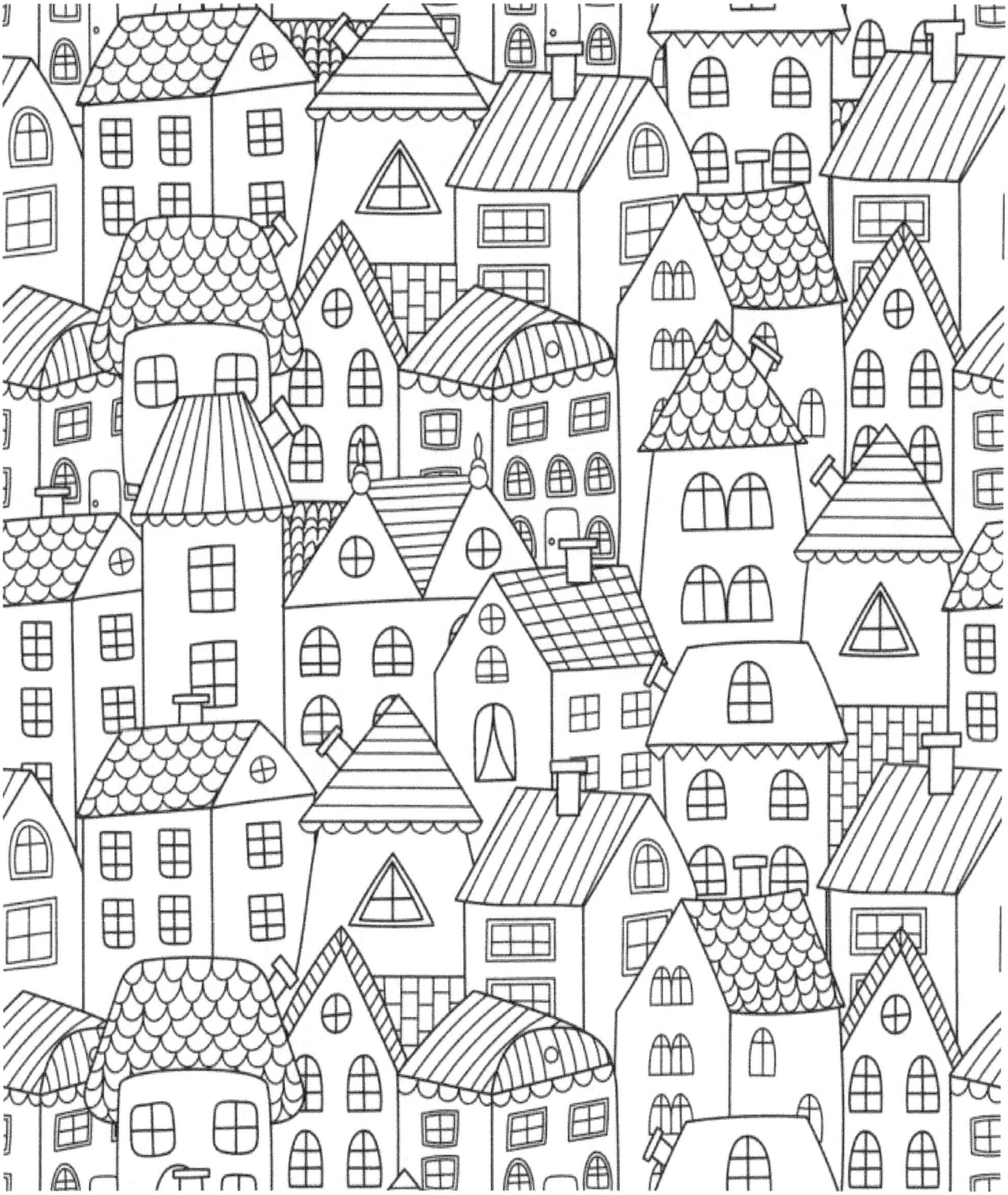

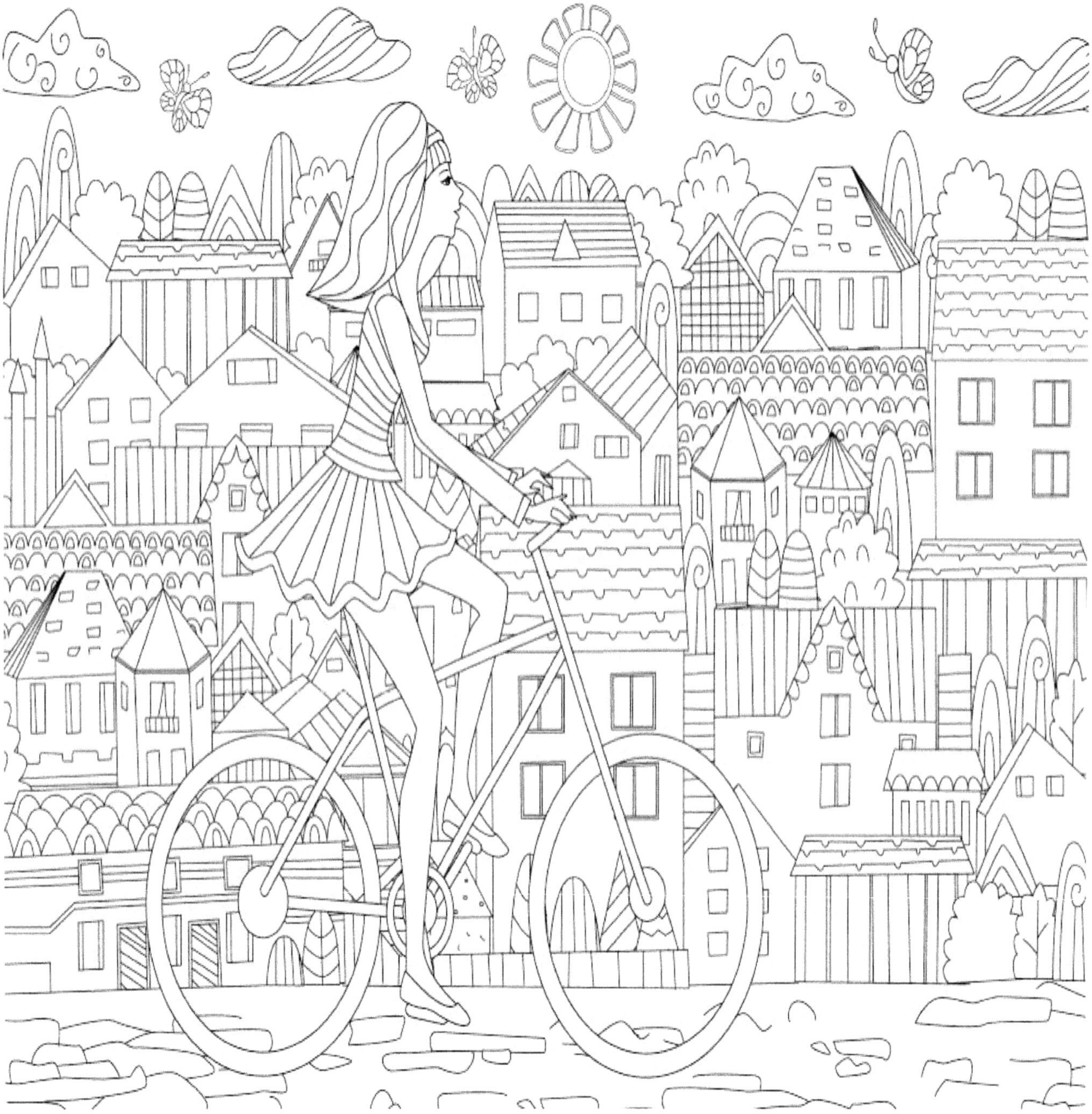

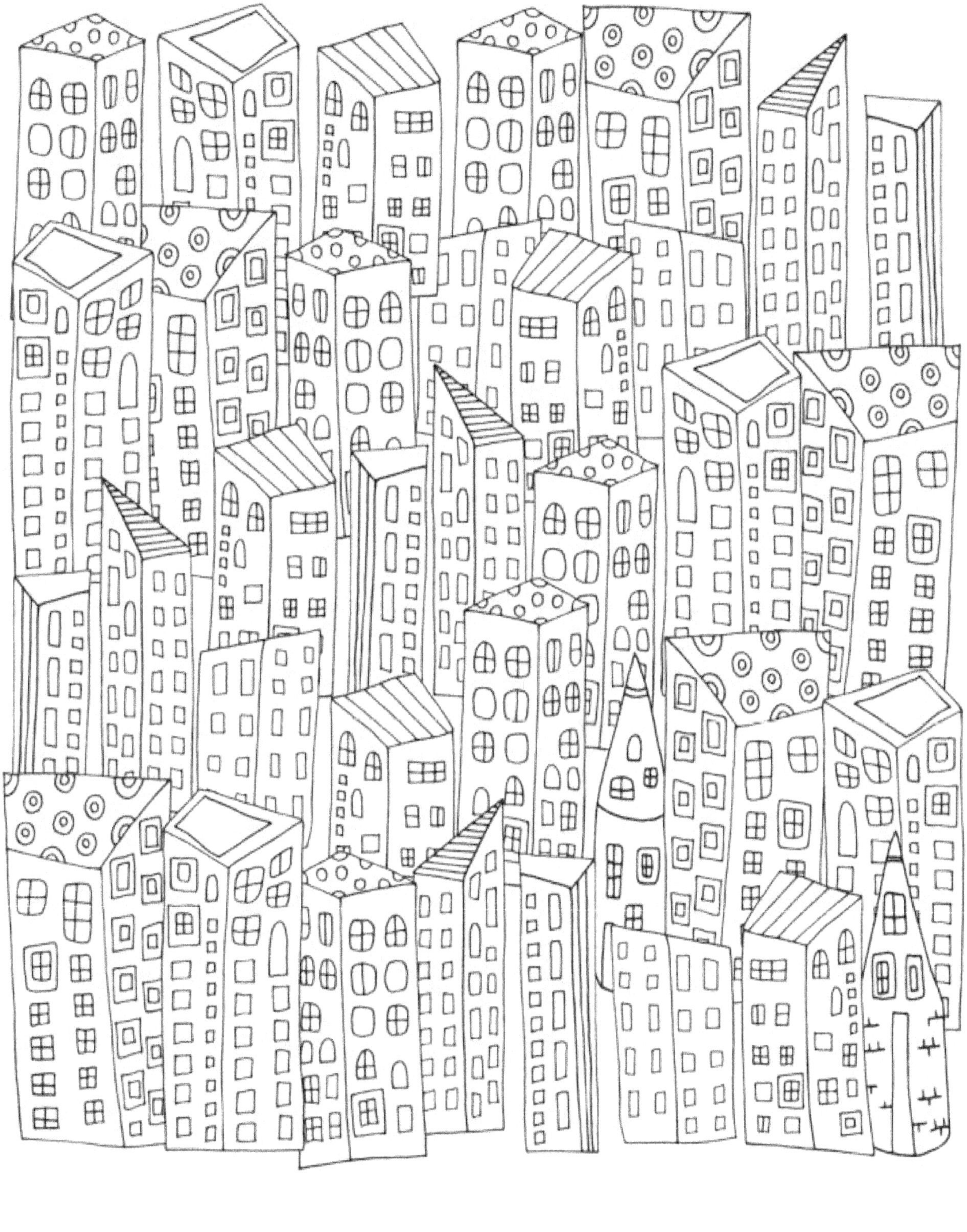

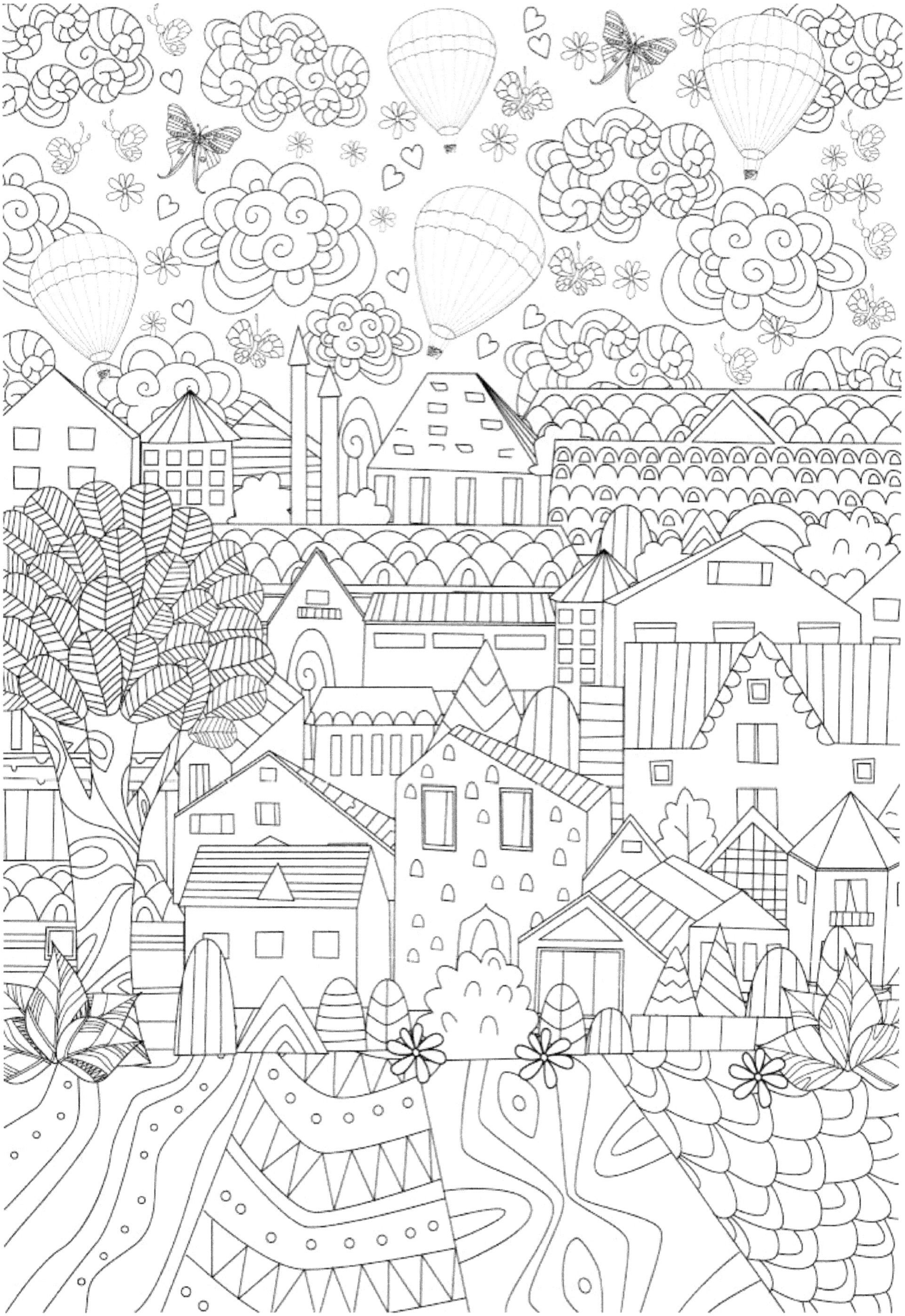

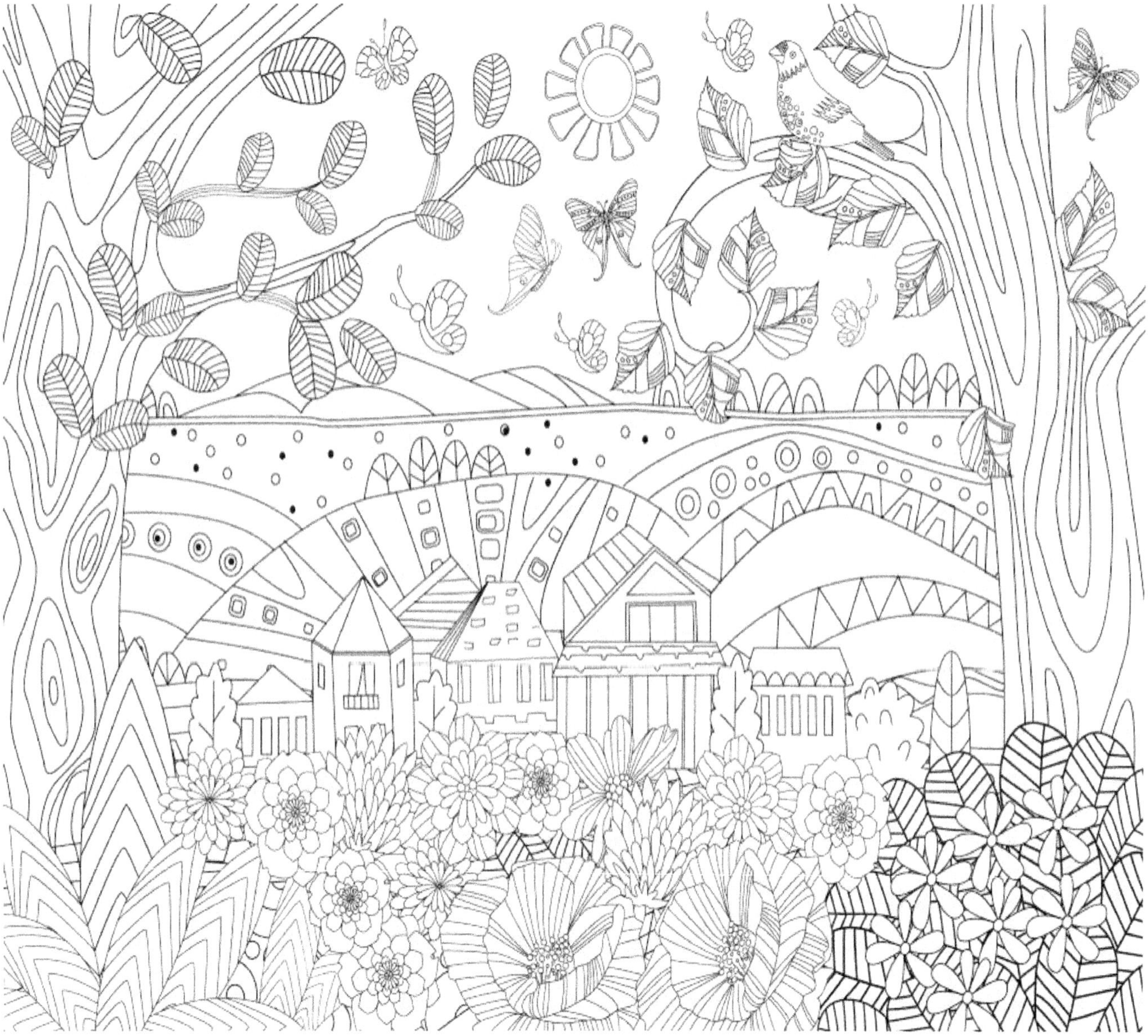

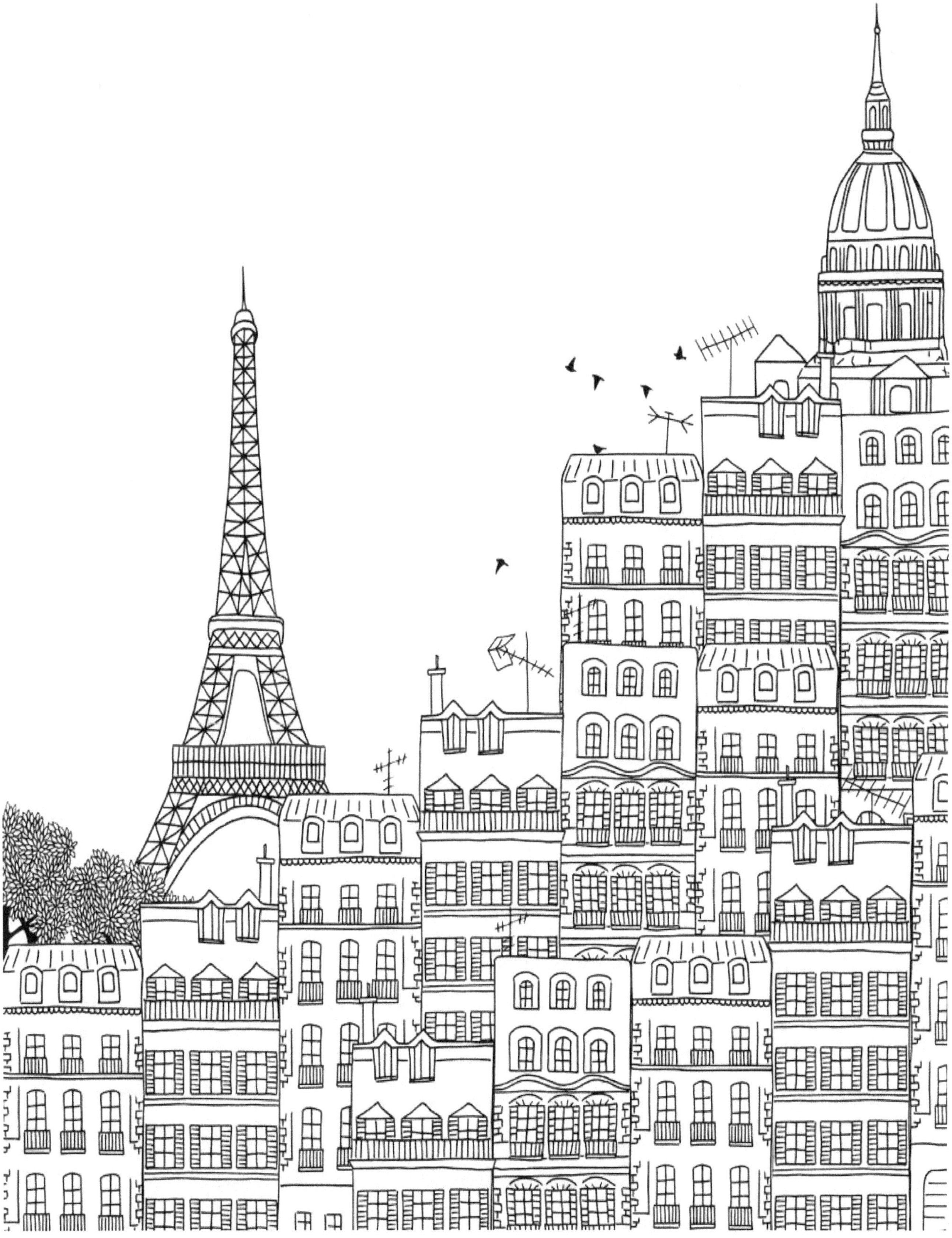

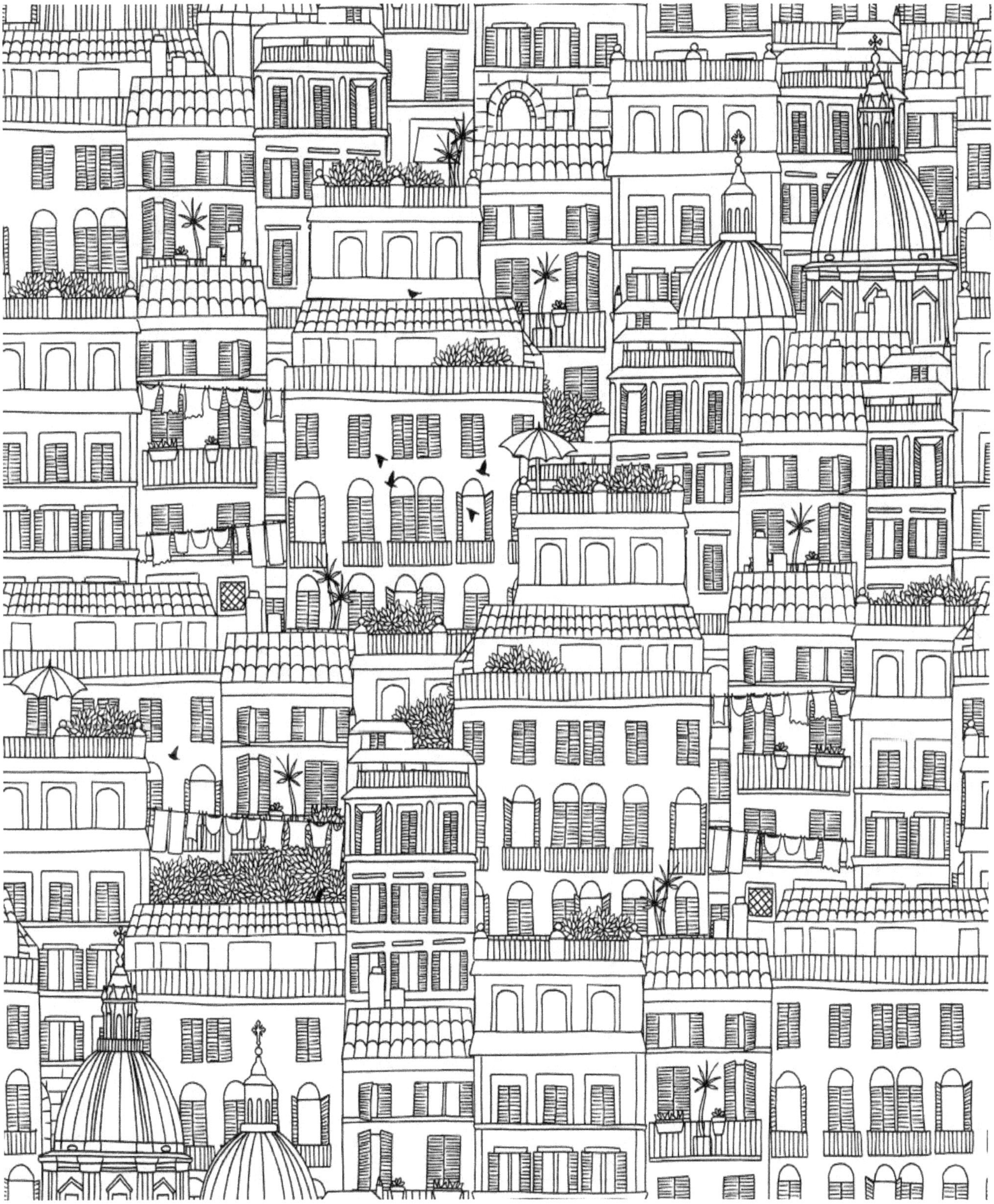

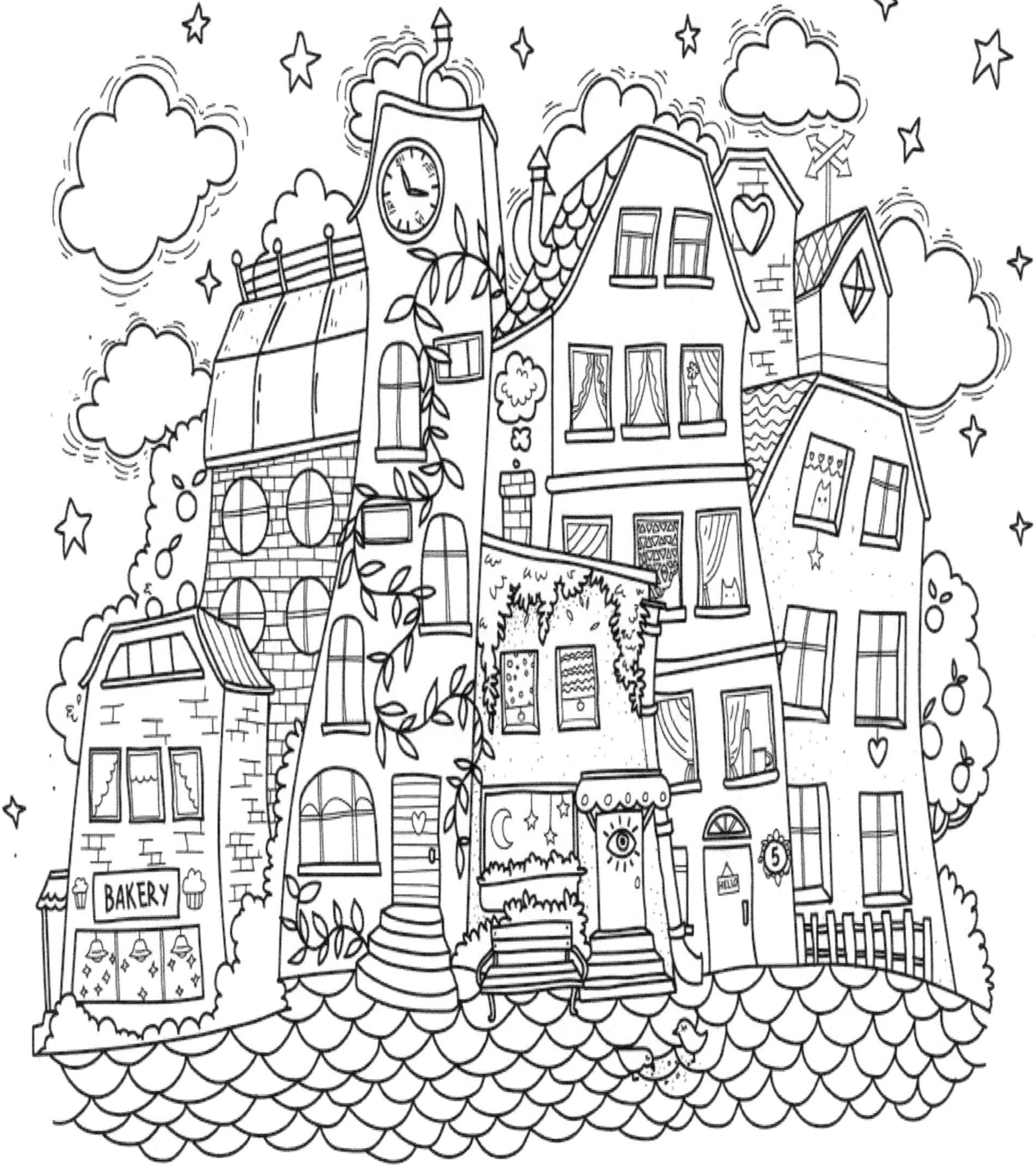
BAKERY
5
HELLO

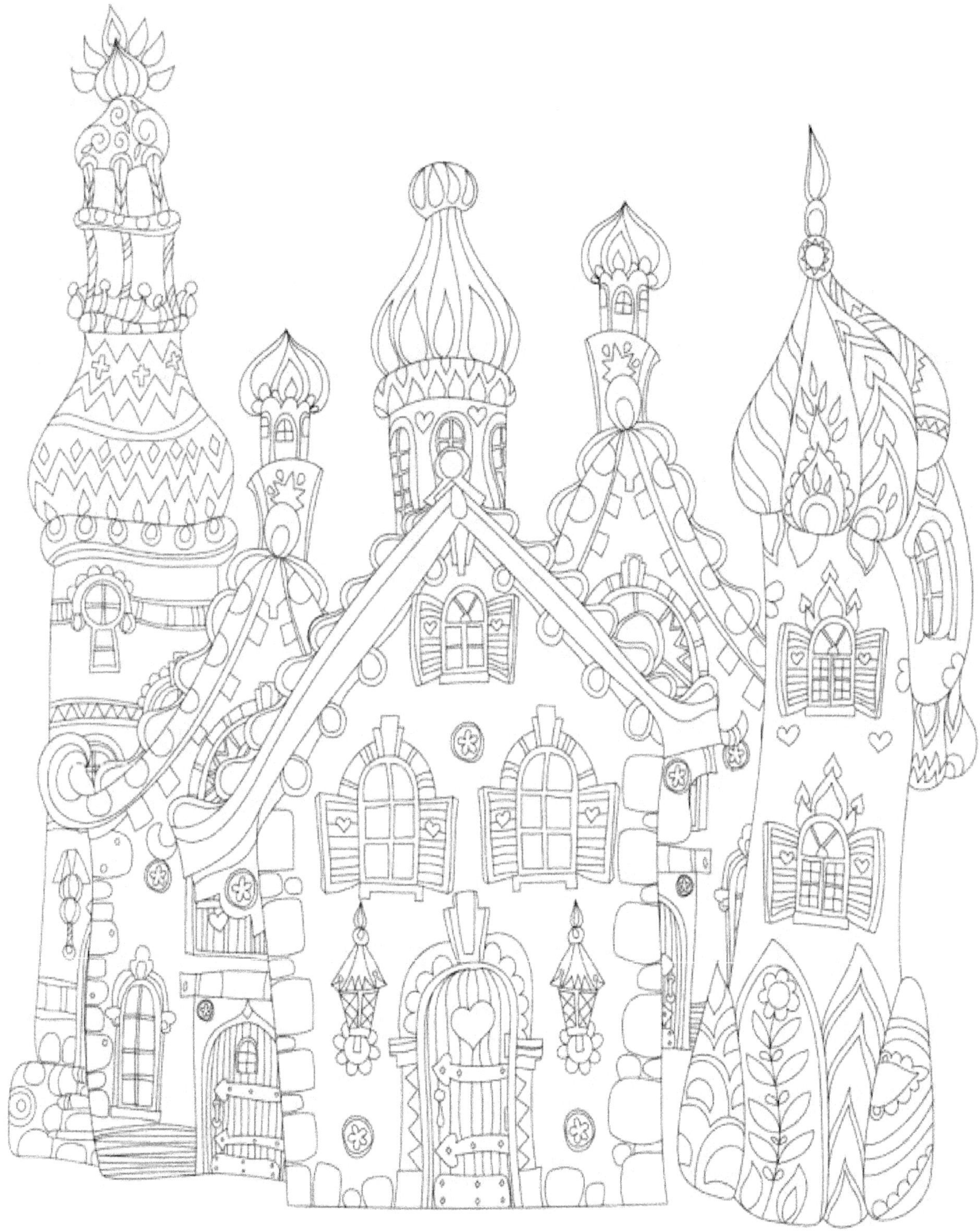

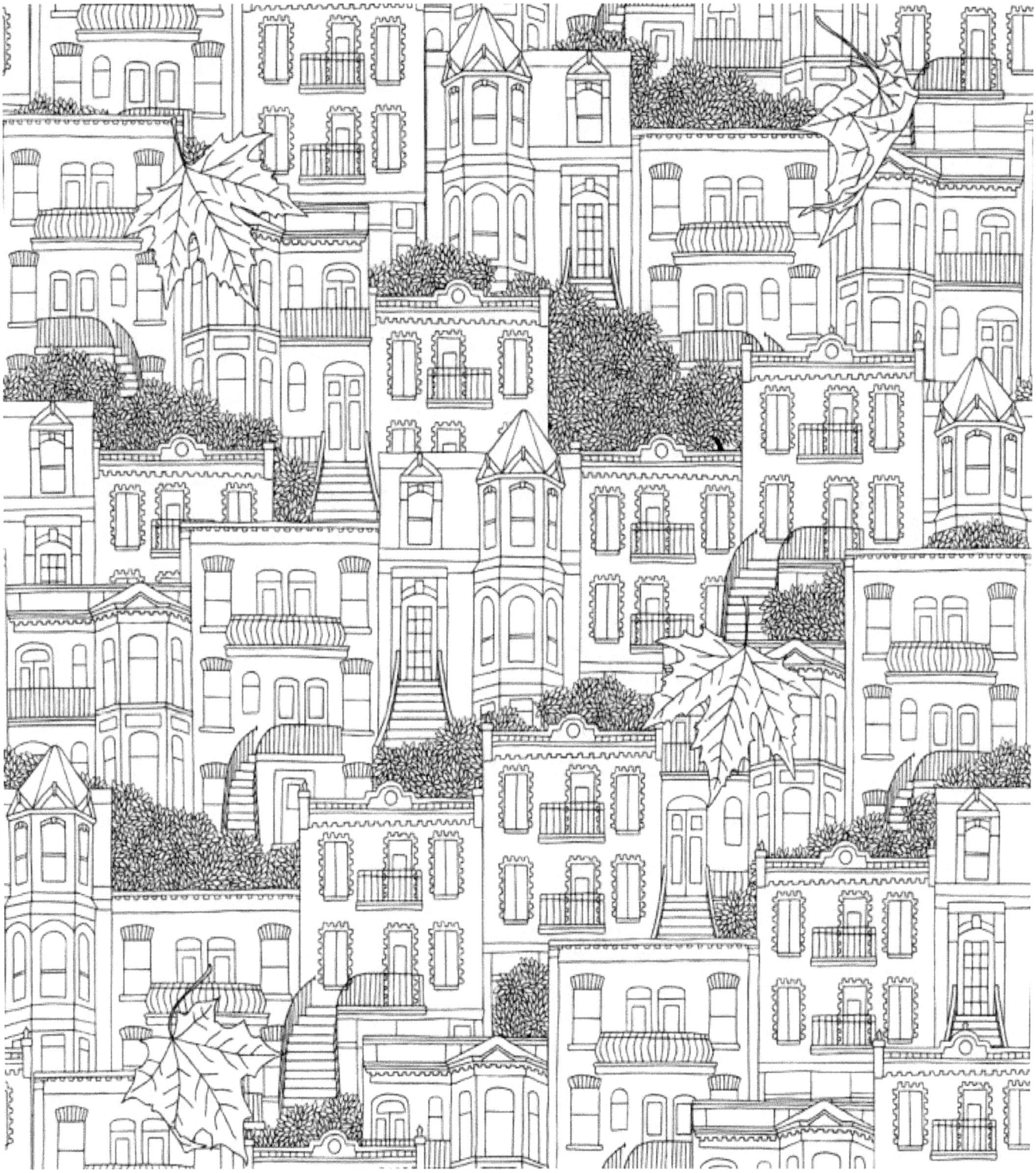

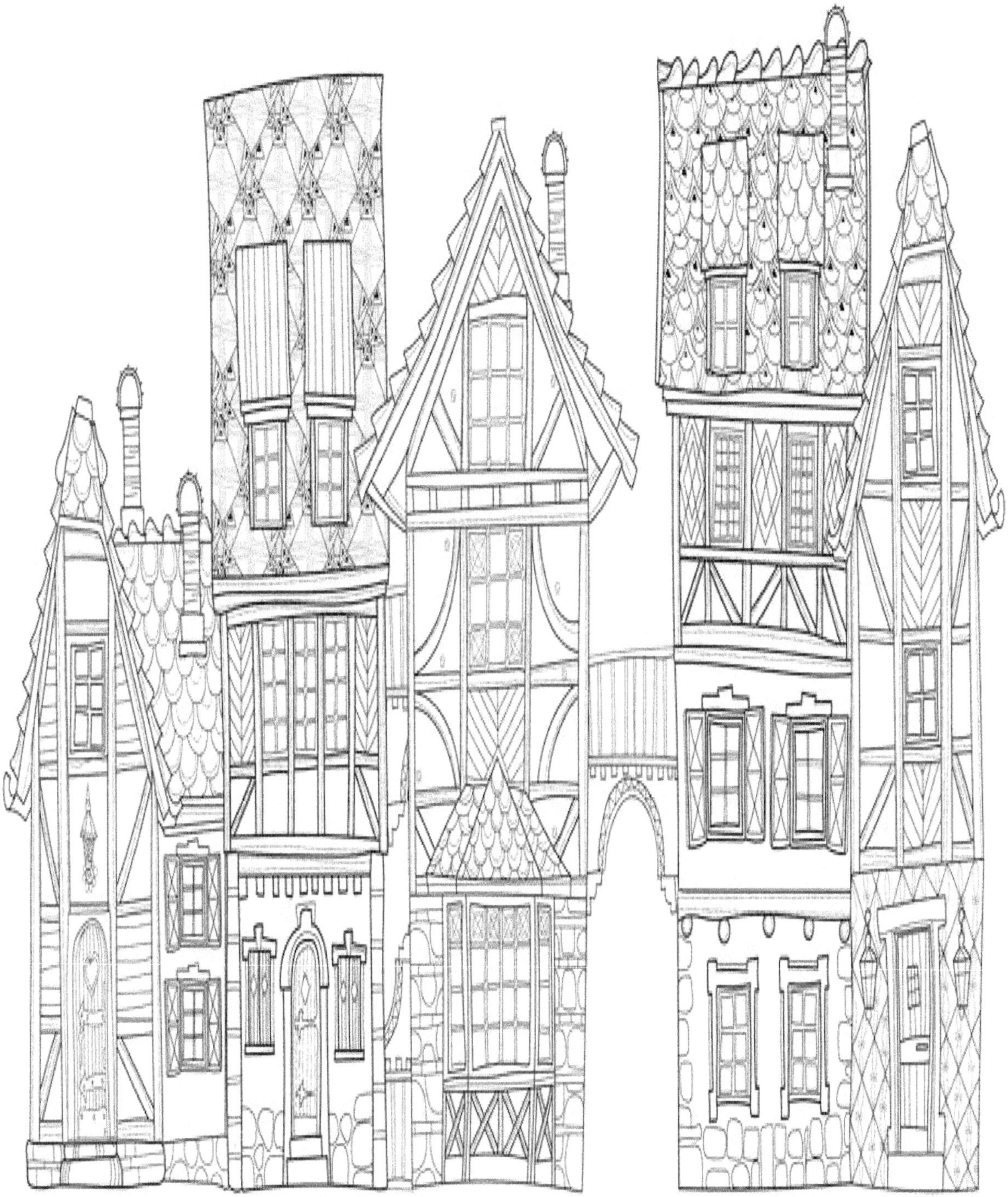

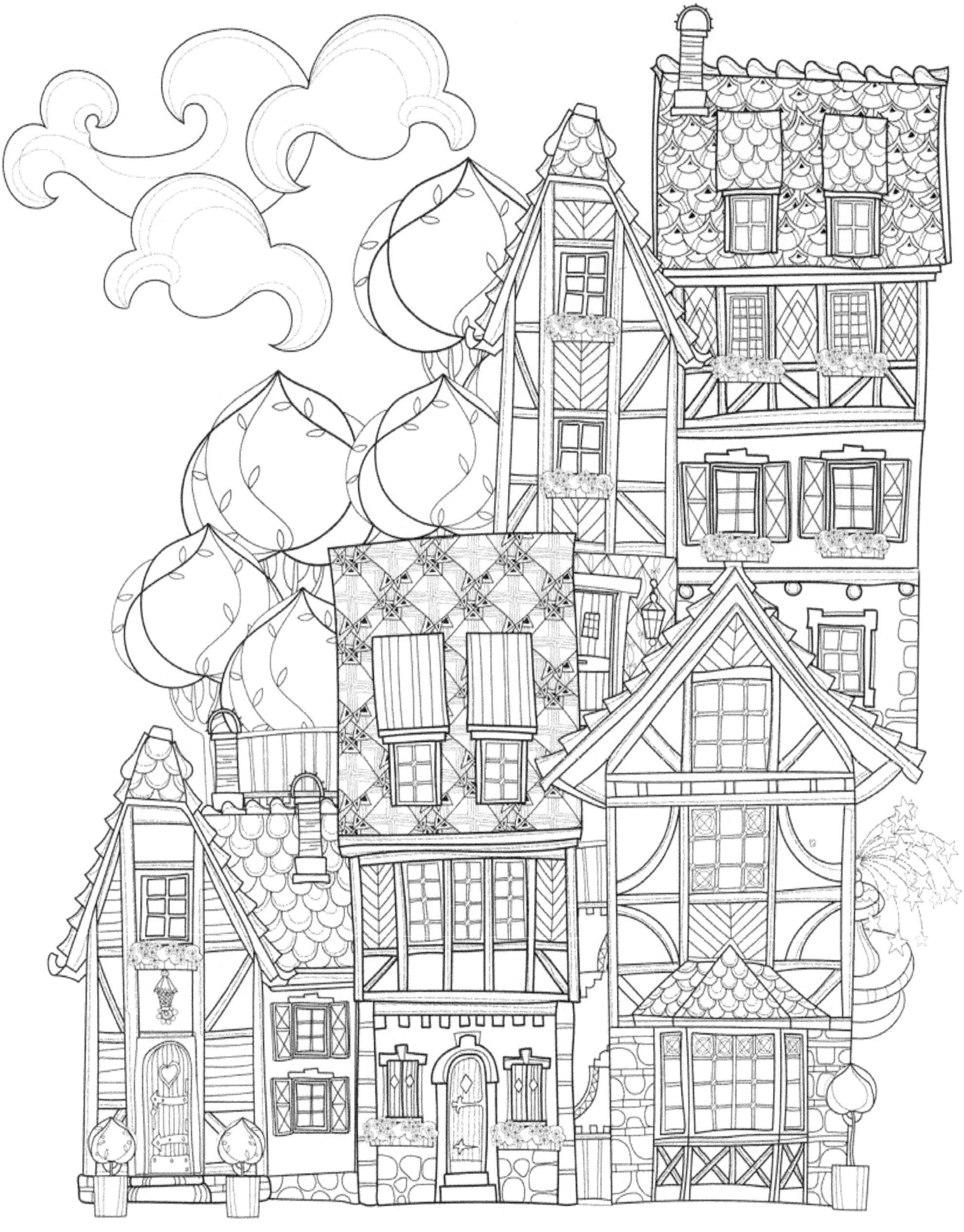

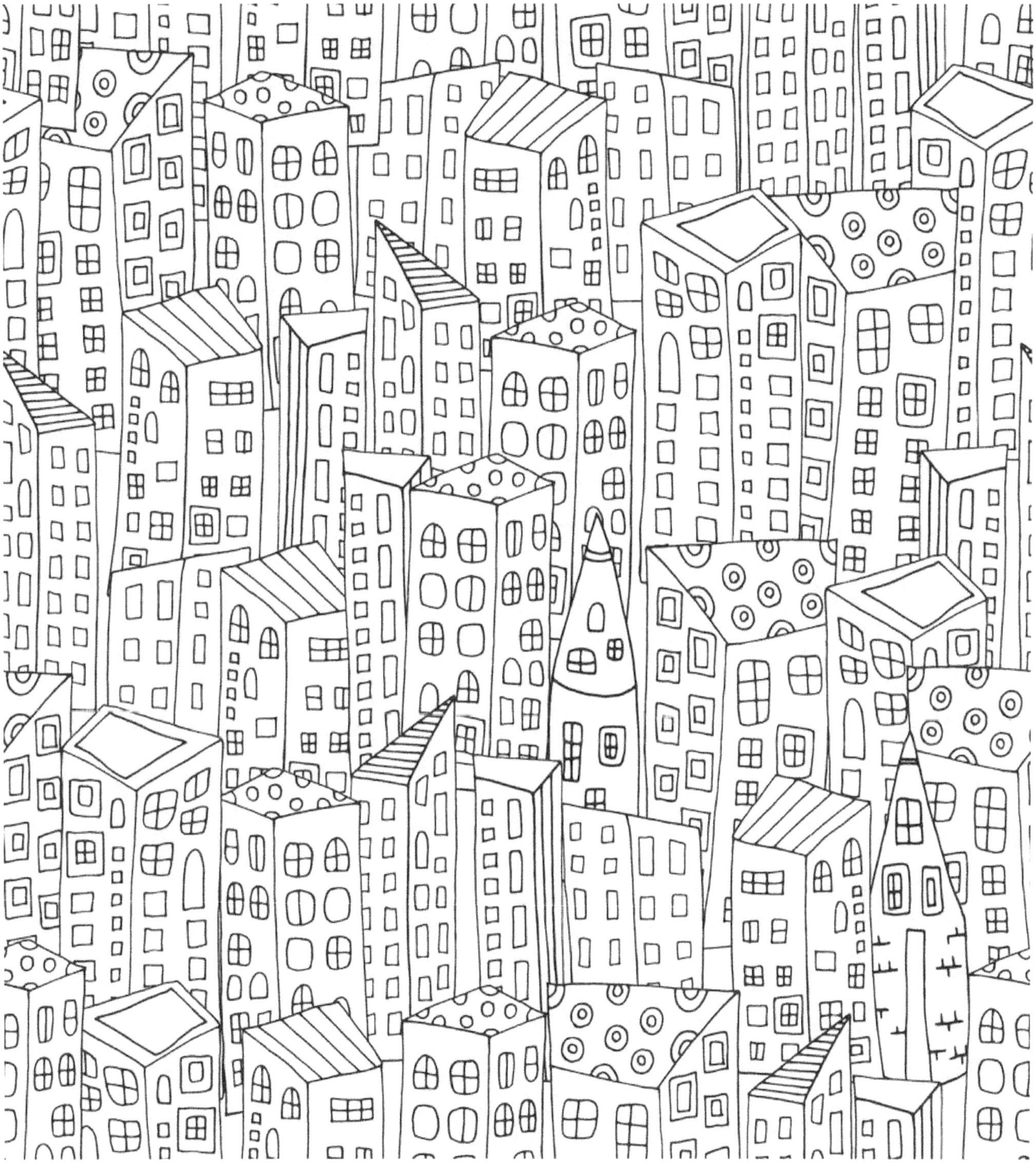

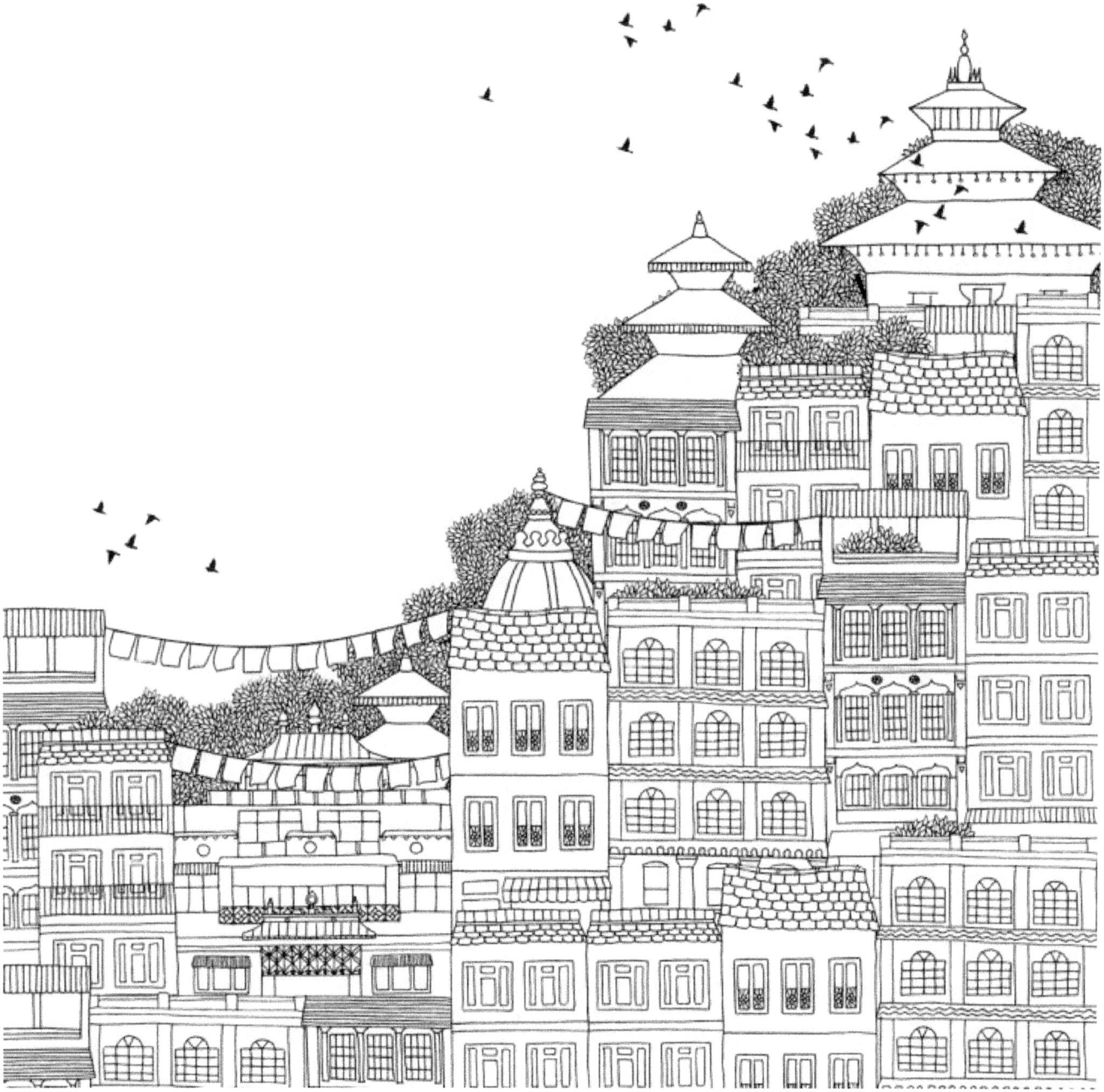

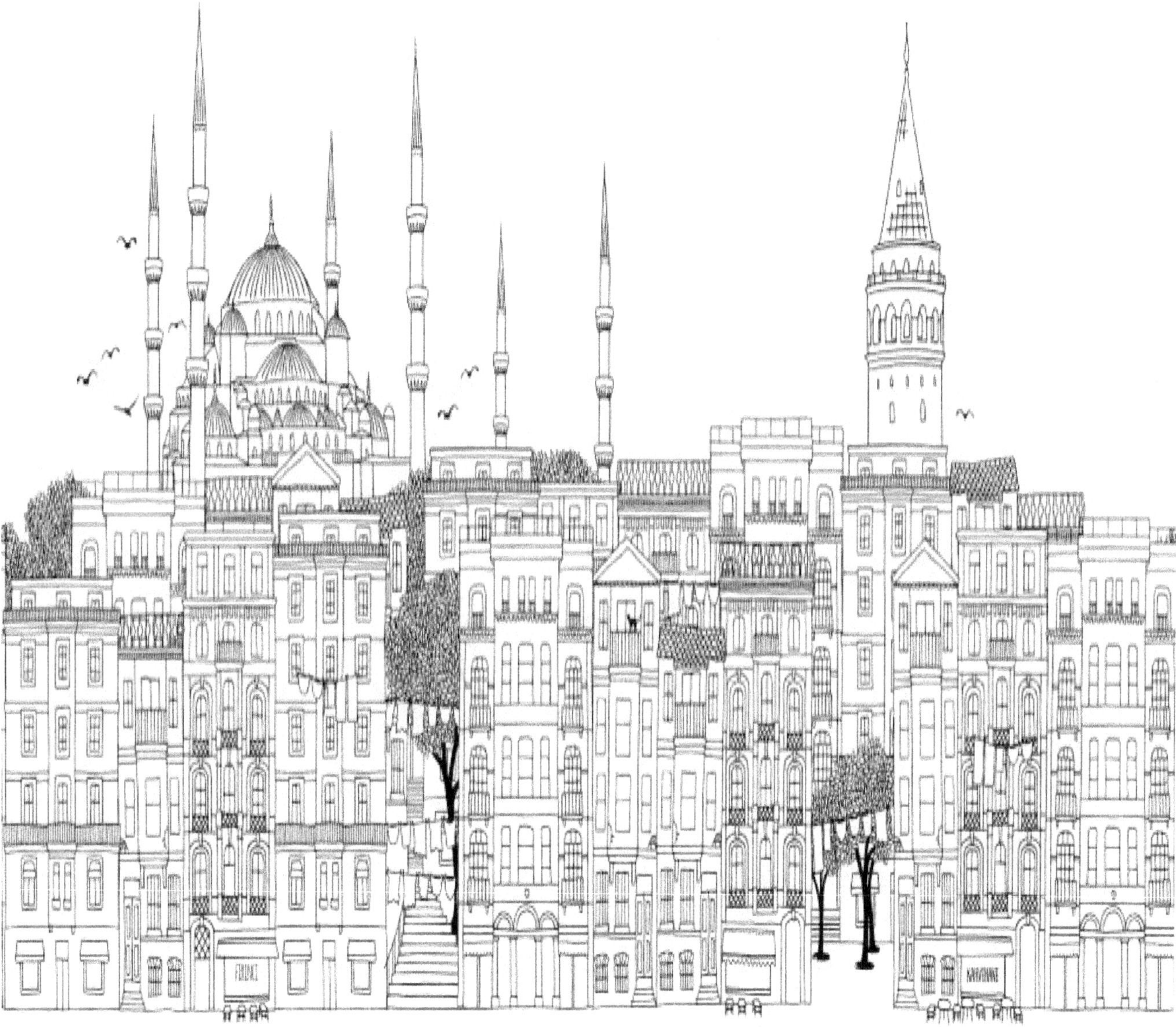

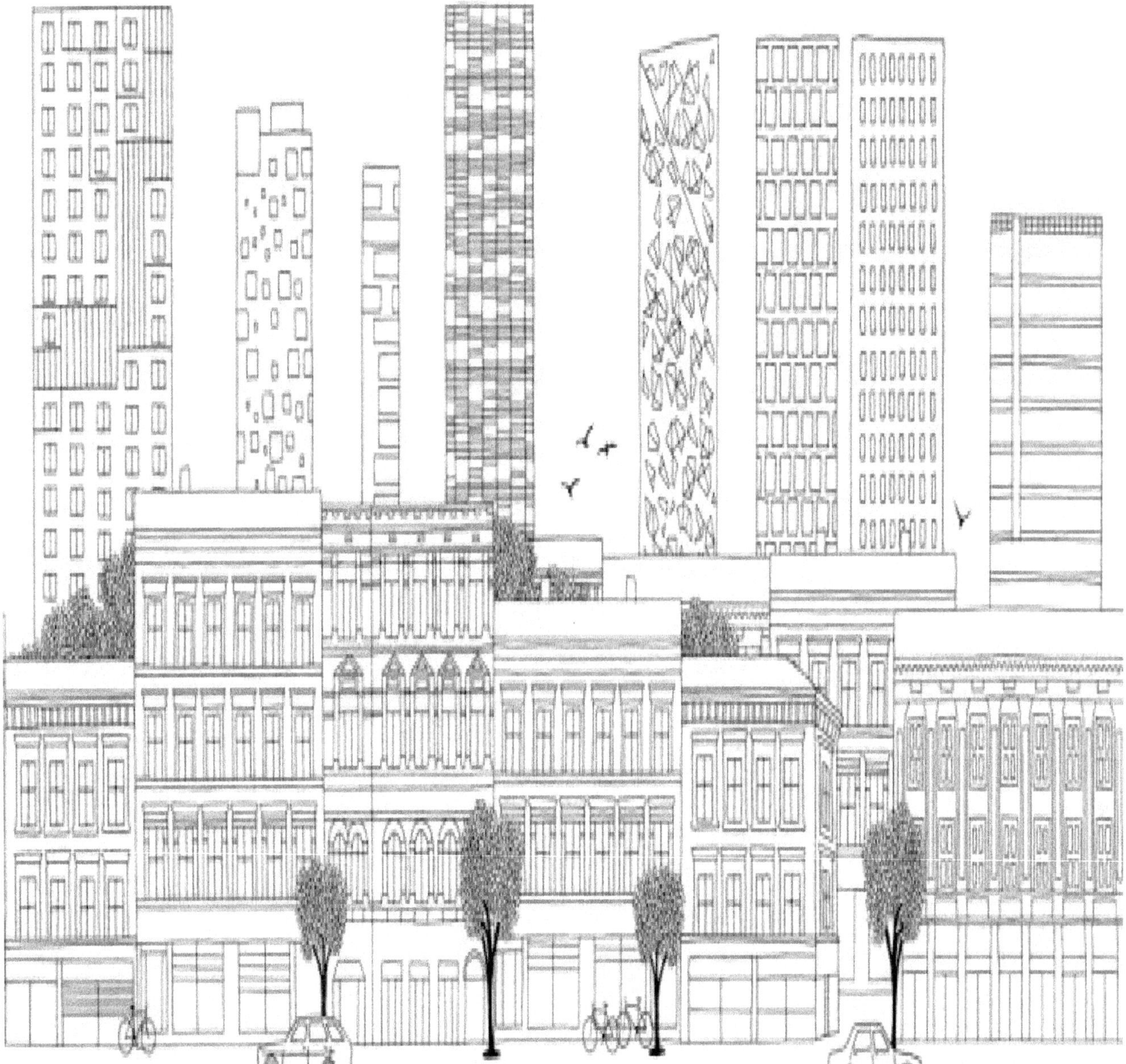

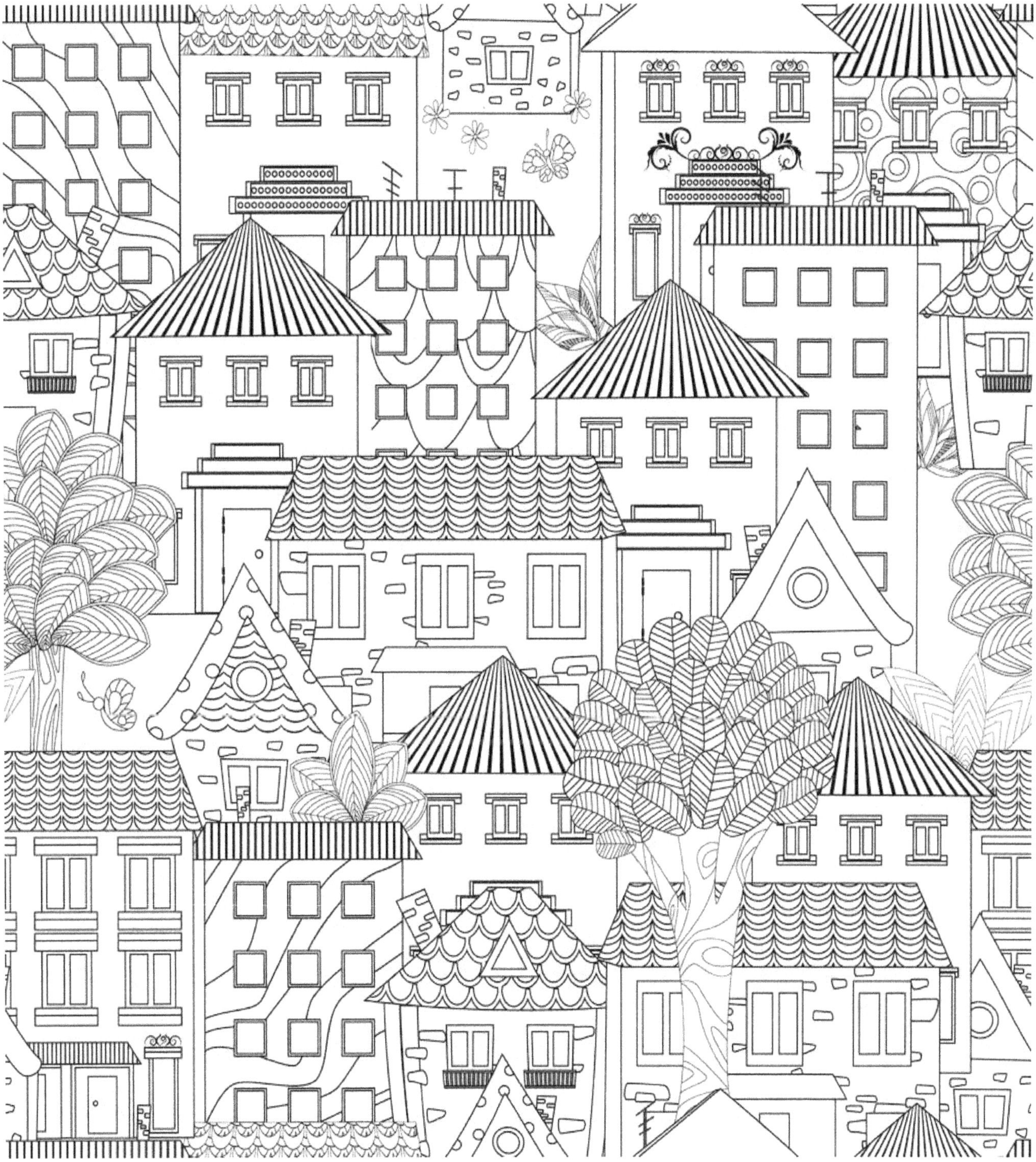

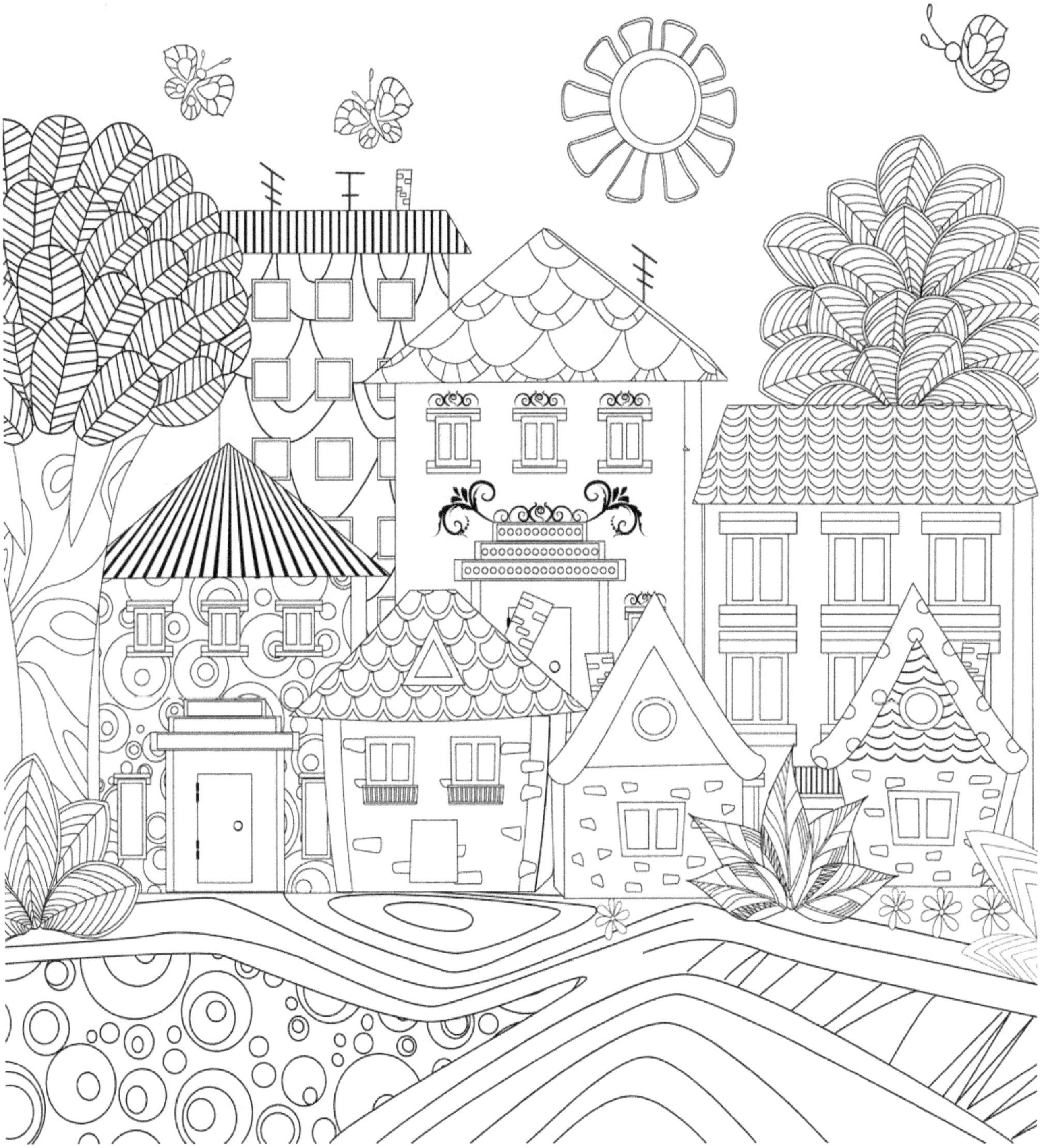

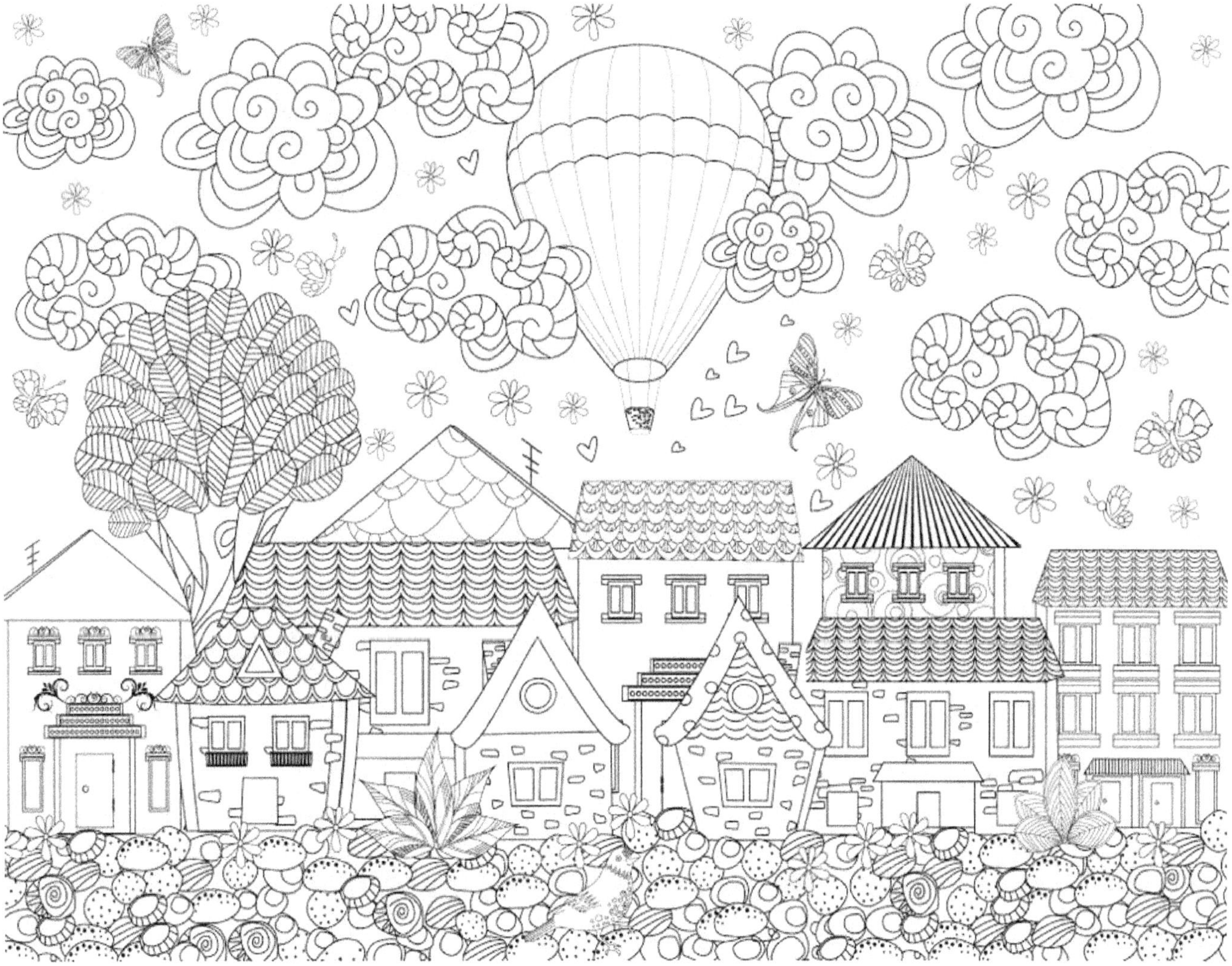

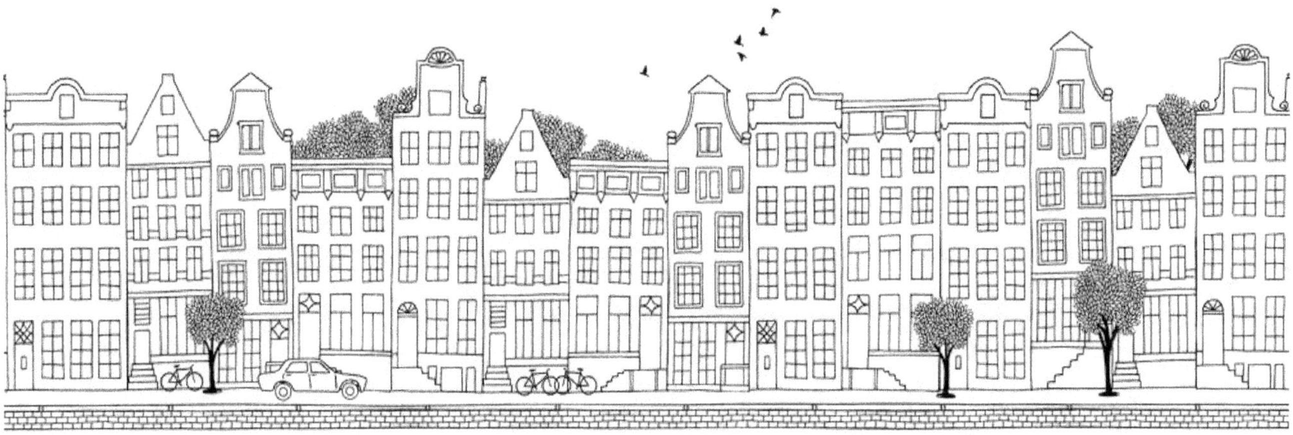

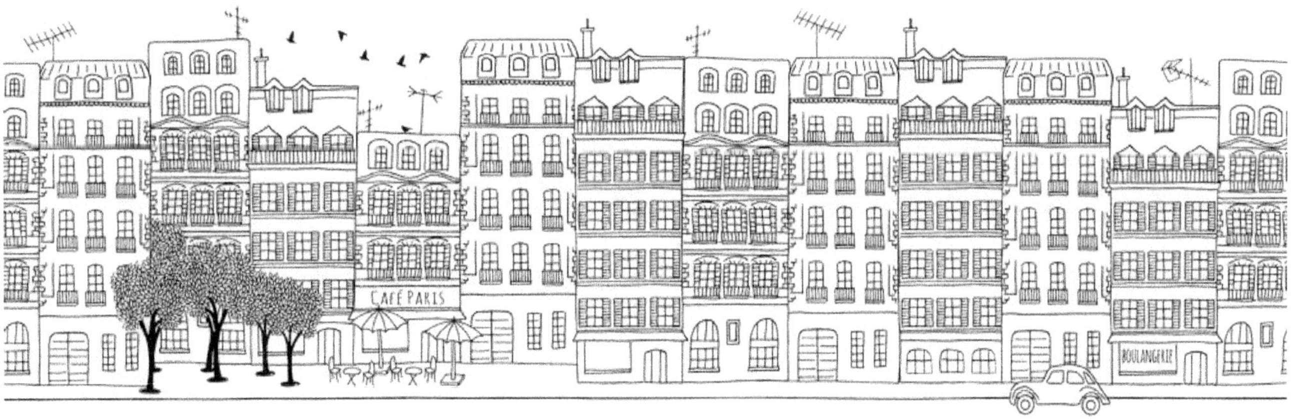
CAFÉ PARIS
BOULANGERIE

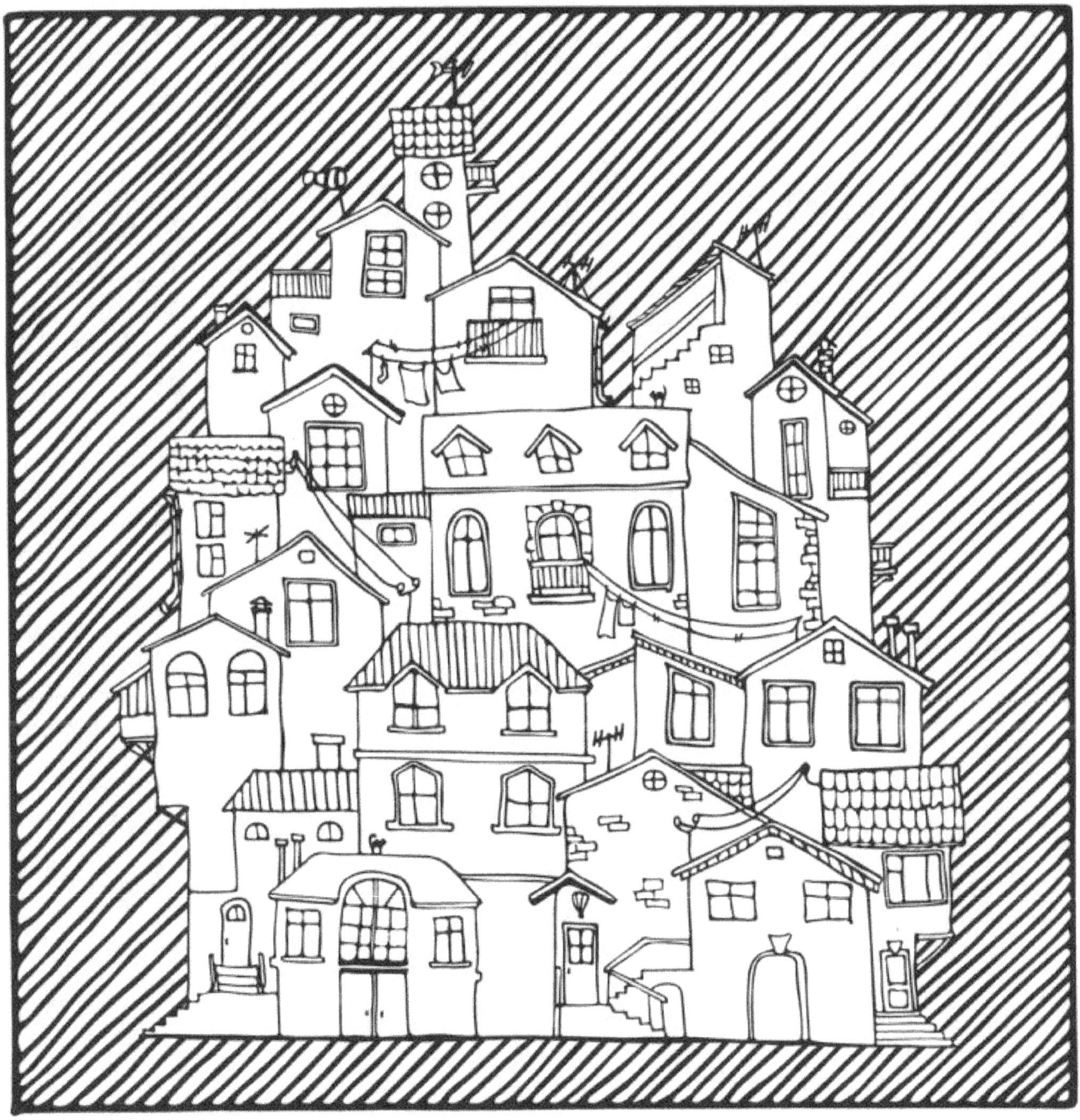

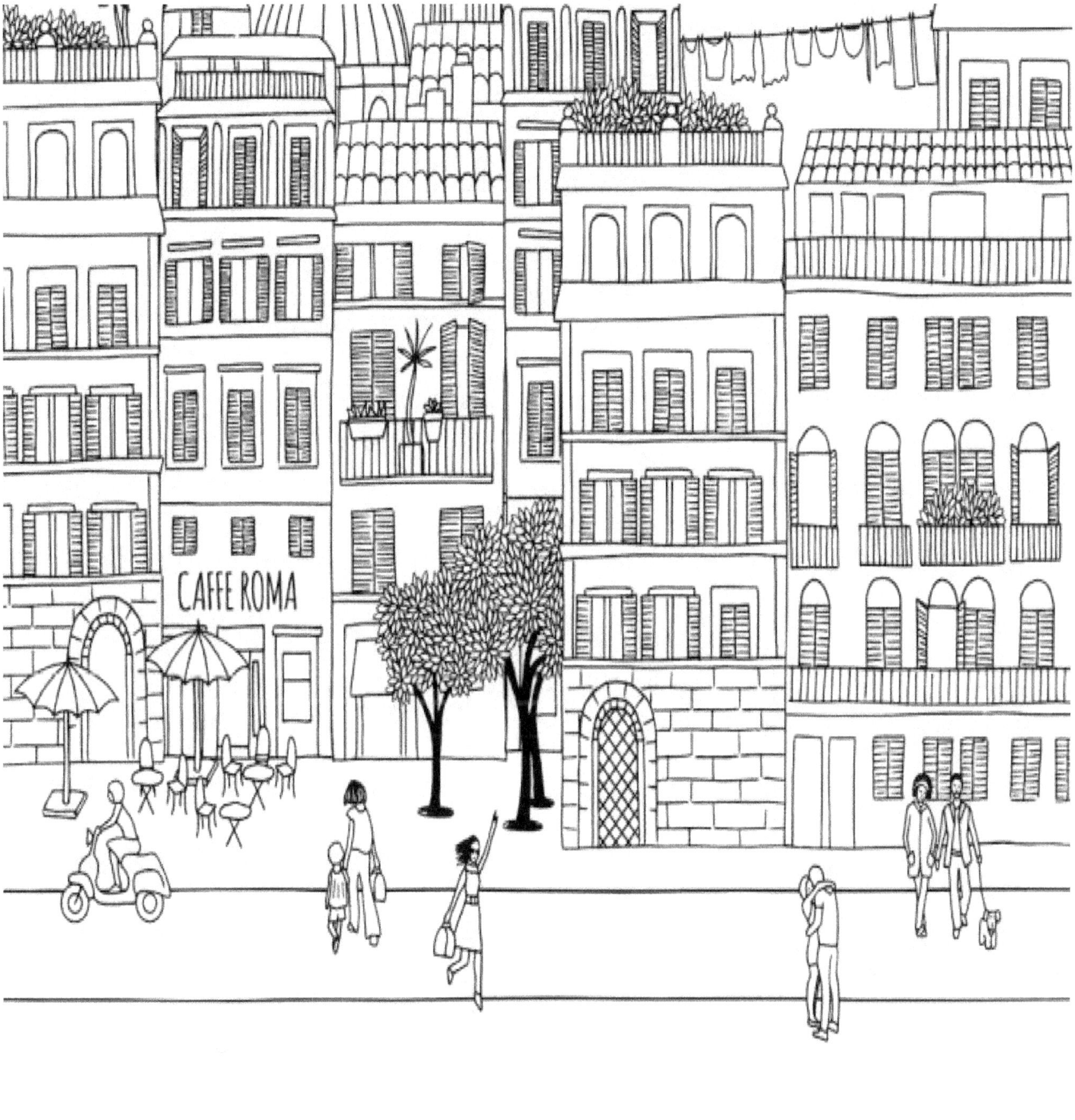
CAFFE ROMA

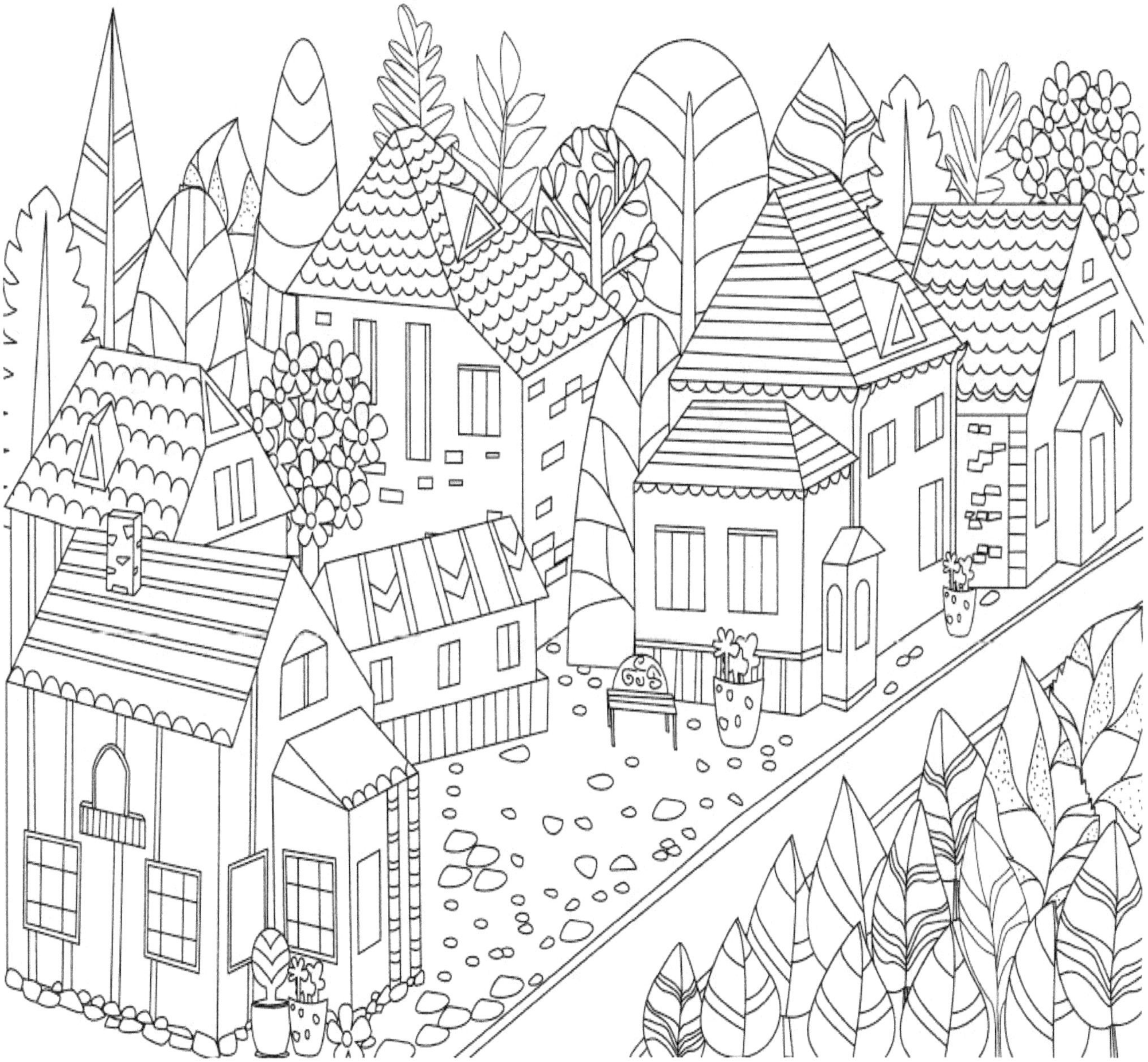

www.ingramcontent.com/pod-product-compliance
Lightning Source LLC
Chambersburg PA
CBHW081524220526
45467CB00010B/3029